BUSTING LOOSE

FROM THE MONEY GAME

BUSTING LOOSE

FROM THE MONEY GAME

MIND-BLOWING STRATEGIES FOR CHANGING THE RULES OF A GAME YOU CAN'T WIN

ROBERT SCHEINFELD

WILEY

John Wiley & Sons, Inc.

CONTENTS

FOREWORD

Throughout history, across ages and generations, there have been beliefs and assumptions that people of the time accepted as true and never questioned for their ultimate truthfulness or accuracy.

Then, later in history, it turned out many of those beliefs and assumptions *weren't* true, so people had to revise their views of the world and adopt a new set of beliefs and assumptions.

For example, there was a time when people thought the world was flat. But we later found out that was wrong.

There was a time when people thought the Earth was at the very center of the Universe and everything else revolved around *us*. But we later found out that was wrong, too.

If you study the history of the medical profession, you find all kinds of beliefs and assumptions about how the body works, what disease is, and how to heal the body that we later found out were false.

If you study science, whatever branch you choose—physics, chemistry, biology, astronomy, and so on—you see the same pattern repeating. You see a stream of beliefs, assumptions, and models scientists were once absolutely certain were truthful and accurate, but which later turned out to be false. As a result, scientists constantly revise their theories and models.

So presumably, if history is any guide, most of what we take for granted about the world simply isn't true. But in any given age or generation, we get so locked into the prevailing beliefs and assumptions (without even realizing it) that we often blind ourselves to The Truth.

One of the largest sets of beliefs and assumptions we've all accepted as true and never questioned is what Bob calls *The Money Game*. The beliefs and assumptions underlying The Money Game have been in place for as long as there has been money. In fact, they may have survived—fully intact—longer than any other set of beliefs and assumptions in history. You could say The Money Game has been something of a sacred cow.

In Chapter 1, Bob discusses the beliefs, assumptions, rules, and regulations underlying The Money Game. As you participate in that discussion, it will seem perfectly normal and reasonable to believe they're all truthful and accurate. "Of course that's how it works," you'll probably say to yourself.

However, as you'll soon see, none of the rules and regulations you've been taught about The Money Game, and none of the beliefs and assumptions underlying those rules and regulations are true—no matter how natural, logical, or reasonable they may seem at first blush.

I've spent most of my life playing The Money Game. In fact, I started playing it at the age of 10 when I began a newspaper route in my neighborhood. Six months later, I began pumping spring water into gallon jugs at a nearby park and delivered the water to the homes of neighbors in my wagon.

I later became a masterful player of The Money Game. However, as Bob says, "No matter how well you play it, and no matter how much money you pile up as you play, there's always a major price to pay in the form of stress, anxiety, pain, loss of something else that's important to you, or disillusionment—if you play according to the rules, regulations, and structure you're taught growing up."

In my own life, despite numerous achievements I'm very proud of, like the *Chicken Soup for the Soul*® series having sold 100 million copies in 41 languages around the world, a Guinness book world record, and numerous honors and awards, and despite being able to accumulate lots of money, I always did pay a big price, like the many times I spent six or more tiring months on the road, away from family and friends, launching a new book series or other project.

As a result, like Bob and so many others, the better I got at playing The Money Game, the more I noticed a growing desire to find a new way of playing and a new set of rules that would still enable me to create and experience abundance, but also empower me to wrap it up in a decidedly different package—*with zero price to pay!*

When the time comes for an old set of beliefs and assumptions to give way to a new one, it always starts out with a single individual saying "No, that's not right. This is what's true." Invariably, that individual is resisted, criticized, even attacked viciously. But a few people still listen and see The Truth, then a few more, then a few more, until it reaches a critical mass. Then the old way of thinking collapses and the new way of thinking explodes into mass consciousness.

My prediction is that the transformational insights and Busting Loose Process you're about to discover will be the start of a revolution that ultimately collapses the old beliefs and assumptions about abundance and The Money Game and creates a worldwide explosion of new possibility and opportunity.

Interestingly enough, although Bob is a lone voice speaking about a new Truth at the moment, he's not being resisted, criticized, or attacked. Quite the contrary. People all over the world are resonating with his message of an alternative to the traditional Money Game and joyously exploring a new way of creating and experiencing total abundance.

Have you ever said words like these to yourself: "I wish someone had told me that a long time ago?" If so, you know what it's like to discover something that radically changes your life in the blink of an eye. As you prepare to read this book, take a deep breath, buckle your seatbelt, and get ready to blink!

JACK CANFIELD, CEO
Chicken Soup for the Soul Enterprises;
co-creator of the *Chicken Soup for the Soul*® series;
co-author of *The Success Principles*™: *How to Get from Where You Are to Where You Want to Be*

ACKNOWLEDGMENTS

This book could never have been written without the help, influence, and inspiration of many people. It's not possible to thank everyone who contributes to a work of this scope, but I'd like to make special mention of a number of people.

First, I'd like to express my appreciation for my good friend and mentor B. W., a master player of The Human Game who took me under his wing and supported me brilliantly, beautifully, and magnificently as I moved deeper and deeper into Phase 2. He's an intensely private man and per our agreement, I'm keeping his identity private. However, I could not write this book without acknowledging his contributions to me and what you'll discover in the pages that follow.

Second, words can't possibly express the appreciation I feel for Arnold Patent who reminded me of many extremely powerful puzzle pieces and supported me so beautifully in opening up to who I really am. Arnold, I'll be eternally grateful!

I'd also like to express my appreciation for my friend Dr. John Demartini who helped open my eyes and primed the pump for my understanding of many of the scientific insights I share with you.

I'd also like to express my appreciation for Amit Goswami, Lynn McTaggart, and Michael Talbot for the puzzle pieces they gave me through their books and the clarity those puzzle pieces helped me reach.

Special thanks must also go to my good friend Dale Novak who did the beautiful illustrations you'll see throughout the book, and Vaughan Davidson, designer extraordinaire, for designing the big, bold, bright image that visually depicts Busting Loose from The Money Game on the cover of this book and on my Busting Loose web sites. If you like his style and need help with covers of any kind or web site design work, you can contact Vaughan at vaughan@killercovers.com.

I must also express my tremendous appreciation to my editor, Richard Narramore, at Wiley for believing in me, believing in this project, getting it approved, and helping me carve the creation you're about to experience.

Finally, I can't utter the word *inspiration* without simultaneously mentioning "Beauty" (my wife Cecily) and my two kids, Ali and Aidan, who inspire me on a daily basis and support me so perfectly in opening up to even more abundance, joyfulness, and appreciation in my life.

INTRODUCTION

What child unable to sleep on a warm summer night hasn't thought he saw Peter Pan's sailing ship in the sky? I will teach you to see that ship.[1]

    —Roberto Cotroneo, *When a Child on a Summer Morning*

Truth has a way of reaching the soul of the seeker, even though the outer garments may temporarily distract the gaze.[2]

                                  —Joseph Whitfield

What I'm about to share with you in this book is going to go against the grain of everything you've learned since childhood, and most likely everything you've believed to be true all your life.

As you read the first seven chapters, you may feel like you've entered the Twilight Zone or a science fiction movie. You may also have thoughts like these:

- "What does this have to do with money?"
- "Get to the point, will you?"
- "Is he crazy?"
- "He can't be serious!"
- "This isn't what I expected when I bought this book!"
- "No way!"

Or my personal favorite:

- "Bullshit!"

You may chuckle, but please take these words seriously because in a few short minutes (if you continue reading right now), thoughts like that may come up for you and I don't want them to distract you or delay your progress toward busting loose from The Money Game.

You may feel, at times, overwhelmed, disoriented, skeptical, angry, or uncomfortable. That's all to be expected. You can't bust loose from The Money Game without a radical shift in your perceptions about yourself, other people, the world, and the strategies you use on a daily basis. The process of making a radical shift like that pushes all kinds of buttons. That's why I subtitled this book: *Mind-Blowing Strategies for Changing the Rules of a Game You Can't Win!*

However, if you're like most people I speak with about the Busting Loose Process, no matter how much resistance you may feel from one part of yourself, another part will be whispering to you, "That's true and somehow I've always known it." No matter how far "out there" what I'll be sharing may seem at first, the journey I'm going to take you on and the ultimate destination you can reach after taking it are very real. My friend and mentor, whom I refer to as B. W. because he prefers to remain anonymous, busted loose from The Money Game. I busted loose myself into the new way of living I describe in Chapter 13, and I've been quietly teaching others from around the world to do it, too. Busting loose is very real and very possible for you to do also.

If you follow the action steps I give you at the end of the book and you still want or need it, you'll be able to get all the proof you want of the truthfulness and validity of what I share from your own experiences. This is a key point I'll be discussing in greater detail in later chapters.

This book has six sections:

1. Background on how I made the discovery and breakthrough that led to it.

2. The Rules of The Game.

3. The philosophy that opens the door to busting loose from The Money Game.

4. The science that documents and validates the philosophy.

5. The specific, practical, simple, yet incredibly powerful action steps flowing out of that philosophy and science that can be taken to transform your life and finances in ways you can't even imagine right now. In this section, I'll also be sharing real world stories to illustrate what everything I shared in the philosophy and science segments looks and feels like.

6. An Invitation for you to take a leap of faith, apply what you discover here, prove its validity and power to yourself, and open up to a new and radically different way of life.

We'll begin with the background in this Introduction. Please go back now and re-read step number five before you continue. Why? Because it's going to take me a while to go through the philosophy and science that make the practical action steps possible. You may feel impatient for me to "get to the meat" from time to time. I want you to remember we're ultimately headed for extremely practical application in your daily life. And I promise you that when we get to the practical aspects of the Busting Loose Process, you'll understand and be extremely grateful for the foundation I laid to make them possible.

Many people who enter my orbit and discover what you're about to discover in this book, ultimately ask me "Where did you get this stuff?" I reply by saying this:

> The only way I can answer you is to compare it to the assembly of a jigsaw puzzle. You take a piece here, a piece there, another piece here, another piece there. By themselves, they don't look like much, but as you assemble more and more pieces, the big picture

starts to come into view. Then, as more and more pieces get assembled, the complete picture ultimately pops into clear view. No one person or source gave me all the pieces, but I kept searching for, collecting, and assembling the pieces. Then, one day, the complete picture you're about to discover popped into view—and blew me away, as it'll blow you away if you allow it to.

The first puzzle pieces came from the amazing grandfather I had growing up. His name was Aaron Scheinfeld. He took a simple idea and turned it into a Fortune 500 company you've probably heard of—Manpower, Inc.—the world's largest temporary help service. As I grew up, I became aware there was something very unusual behind the gigantic success he'd created and the fortune he'd amassed—some mystery about it that either no one in the family knew or they weren't talking about.

When I was 12, every chance I got, I'd pepper him with questions, trying to uncover what the big secret and mystery was. For the better part of a year he put me off. Then, while the extended family was on a trip to Crans, Switzerland, to celebrate my grandfather's 70th birthday, he invited me to join him for a cup of hot chocolate and finally told me his story.

On that day, he started me on the path of understanding two critical Truths that changed my life forever:

1. There are hidden forces driving what happens in the world that few people ever find out about.
2. By understanding and learning to tap those hidden forces, tremendous power can be unleashed and used to create literal miracles in your life.

Books, tapes, and lectures throughout history have been filled with similar messages. But the way my grandfather defined "hidden forces" and the specific ways he went about tapping these forces were very different, so if those words sound familiar, stick with me because I'm going to take them in a decidedly different direction.

Good news and bad news came from that first meeting with my grandfather in the small cafe in Crans, Switzerland. The good news is he began teaching me about the true nature of the hidden forces and mentoring me on how to tap them. The bad news is he died seven months later before he could complete my education. So, I spent 35 years applying what he taught me and following the many clues he left, working diligently to find the missing puzzle pieces and assemble them into the complete system I believe he would have given me had he lived to do so.

During those 35 years, I found many of the missing puzzle pieces. I assembled them into a system I applied to become a master at playing The Money Game. In the early days of my career, I applied the system to become a top salesperson for a computer reseller, and produced extraordinary results as a sales manager, corporate communications manager, regional manager, director of marketing, vice president of marketing, consultant, and entrepreneur.

I later applied the system to create and execute a marketing model that packed rooms at Tony Robbins' multimedia seminars, and fuel the growth of a computer store franchise company called Connecting Point of America from $90 million to $350 million in very profitable sales . . . in less than three years.

As I continued applying my system, I amassed my own fortune, but then crashed and burned and ended up $153,000 in debt. I later recovered and rebuilt my fortune even bigger than before. Among the many projects contributing to my second fortune, I grew Blue Ocean Software from $1.27 million to $44.3 million in just four years, resulting in the company being named three times to *Inc. Magazine's* "Inc. 500" list. That tremendous growth, accompanied by staggering profitability, led to Blue Ocean being acquired by software giant Intuit for $177 million, a substantial chunk of which went into my pocket as a reward for my efforts.

Along that journey, I wrote two bestselling books that revealed the puzzle pieces I'd collected at the time. My first book was *The Invisible Path to Success* and the second was *The 11th Element*.

A year after selling Blue Ocean Software, however, after I'd piled up even more money from a series of business successes that followed it, I watched as large chunks of my wealth started disappearing again. I stopped myself and said, "This doesn't make any sense. There must be something I'm missing here." To use a popular phrase from *Alice in Wonderland* and the movie *The Matrix*, I realized I had to go even deeper down "the rabbit hole."

When I crashed and burned the first time, it was just me. No wife, no kids. Losing everything was excruciatingly painful, but I've always had a high threshold for pain. However, I now had a wife and two children and we'd carved out a life and lifestyle that made us extremely happy. If I crashed and burned again, I knew the pain would be unbearable and would be felt by my family too, so I was scared and became obsessed with finding out what I still didn't know. I went exploring again, absolutely committed to finding the final missing puzzle pieces I believed my grandfather had but which I obviously didn't. Eight months later, I found them, and in the pages of this book, I'll be sharing them with you.

What I discovered through my own experiences and my relationships with hundreds of extremely wealthy people (including some of the wealthiest in the world), is that The Money Game is a game you can't win. As you'll soon see, no matter how well you play it, and no matter how much money you pile up while playing, The Money Game always leads to "failure" in the form of stress, anxiety, pain, loss of some kind, or disillusionment—if you play according to the rules, regulations, and structures you were taught growing up.

It doesn't work to simply play The Money Game better and pile up more and more money, which is what most of the experts out there teach. You have to actually bust loose from The Money Game *entirely* and start playing a new game with a new set of rules and regulations of *your* choosing. That's when things truly transform, *stay transformed*, and life gets really exciting!

One more key point before we move on. When reading books, some people start at the beginning and read to the end, sequentially. Others skip ahead, jump around, skim parts and dip down and read other parts. My intent is to support you in busting loose from The Money Game. To do that, I have to give you specific puzzle pieces in a specific order and support you in assembling them in a specific way.

If you follow my lead, a magnificent "big picture" will pop into view and you'll be empowered to bust loose from The Money Game. If you don't, you'll be left with a bunch of funny-looking pieces of cardboard sitting on a table, you'll short-circuit your access to real power, and you'll stay locked in the limitation and restriction of The Money Game. In short, please be patient, read the chapters sequentially at the pace you feel inspired to move, trust me, and follow my lead. I know how to bust you loose from The Money Game and I can help you do it, but only if you follow the map I'm in a unique position to share with you.

You must also understand, from the start, that I can't bust you loose from The Money Game in the pages of this book. I can only show you the way, open the portal to a new world, help you jump through the portal, and show you what to do in the new world you find on the other side. To actually bust loose from The Money Game, there's work you must do. I'll show you exactly what to do, when and how. I'll offer you tremendous support along the way, but it is a journey and it will take time to reach the ultimate destination. It will also require tremendous commitment, patience, persistence, and discipline on your part to "arrive."

If you make the commitment and do the work, the rewards you'll receive are beyond anything you can possibly imagine right now. I can say without the slightest doubt that once you've busted loose, money will become a total non-issue in your life. You'll never again worry about bills, cash flow, or the balance in your checkbook.

No more asking "Can I afford that?" or "Should I buy that?" No more worrying about the in and out flow of money in your life, about your assets and liabilities, personal income, savings, debt, profits, or taxes.

No more of the confusion, stress, and complexity that come with trying to manage, protect, and grow whatever amount of money you've piled up. No more working your butt off to "make ends meet" or carve out a little pleasure or luxury in your life.

Once you bust loose from The Money Game there will be absolutely no limits or restrictions of any kind for you as it relates to money. No matter how sexy or attractive this may sound to you right now, it isn't even in the ballpark of what really happens and how your life really changes when you bust loose. Busting loose from The Money Game is something you must experience to understand.

I call it The Money *Game* for a very specific reason. To discover that reason and the rules of the Game, please turn the page to begin Chapter 1.

FROM THE MONEY GAME

The Rules of the Game

*Three strikes you're out, being caught off base, committing
an error—those are baseball's rules, rules of that game, but
they don't apply outside the game.*[1]

—J. C.

If you're like most of the people I speak with, you've probably
never thought of money and the pursuit of wealth as a game.
When I talk with people and ask them about it, they generally
say something like this to me: "Money is definitely *not* a game. It's
serious business."

The first step in the *Busting Loose Process* is to really "get" that
everything within your financial world—income, net worth, investments, savings, taxes, expenses, invoices, accounts receivable and
payable, profits, and so on—is part of an amazing, elaborate, gigantic, unique, and complex game. I introduce the basic rules of *The
Money Game* in this chapter and then go into more detail in later
chapters.

If you take a close look, most games have rules, regulations, and a clear structure. They also have definite start and stop times and a clear definition of what it means to win. Everyone who chooses to play a game agrees to follow the rules and regulations and observe that game's structure. This is required to make the game work. Although there's a career and income component to playing games at the professional level, most people play games for the sheer fun and pleasure of doing so. People who enjoy watching games (fans) do so for the same reasons.

For example, football is played with a leather ball that's shaped, sized, and constructed to meet rigid specifications. The playing field is 100 yards long. You play four quarters lasting 15 minutes each. A touchdown is worth six points, kicking the ball through the goalposts after a touchdown is worth one point, a field goal is worth three points, and a safety is worth two points. A first down is 10 yards. You may only have a certain number of players on the field at any given time, and they must each play a specific position. There are rules about what players can and cannot do on the field, and if those rules are broken, the offending team is penalized. The team with the most points at the end of the four quarters (or overtime if the score is tied at the end of regulation time) wins the game.

Baseball is another example. It is played on a field that is a certain shape and size—a diamond. Only nine players per team are allowed on the diamond during play, and like football, each player has a specific position. The game is played with bats, balls, and gloves that meet precise specifications. There are nine innings during which each team is allowed three outs. Batters get four balls and three strikes. The pitcher stands on a slightly elevated mound that is a specific distance from home plate where the batter stands. The bases are specific distances from each other. When a player touches home plate after touching each of the other bases, he earns a "run" or a point. The team with the most runs at the end of nine innings (or extra innings if the teams are tied) wins the game.

Golf is our final example. The golfer plays on a course. There are a certain number of holes, greens, fairways, roughs, sand traps, and water hazards on the course. The player uses clubs with L-shaped metal ends to hit precisely constructed balls into small holes. There are specific rules as to what players can and cannot do while playing, and if the rules are broken, the player is penalized. The player with the lowest number of strokes at the end of the course wins.

If you take a close and objective look at football, baseball, and golf, you see that the rules, regulations, and structures appear completely arbitrary and don't make much sense. Consider this:

- *Football:* Run while holding an inflated piece of leather or throw an inflated piece of leather from one person to another as you try to cross a white line and score points. Or try to kick the piece of leather through two metal posts to score points.
- *Baseball:* Try to hit a round piece of rubber and leather that's coming at you at high speed with a wooden stick. Then, if you hit it and no other player catches it with a big piece of leather wrapped around his hand, you run around trying to touch three square pieces of cloth placed on the ground before touching a final piece of cloth to earn runs.
- *Golf:* Try to hit small rounded pieces of rubber and titanium with L-shaped pieces of metal trying to get the round pieces into tiny shallow holes hundreds of yards away with the fewest possible hits or "strokes."

You see what appears to be the same sort of arbitrariness if you look at the rules, regulations, and structures of other popular games—bridge, Monopoly, pool, chess, checkers, blackjack, and so on. You could easily ask yourself, "How did anyone ever think up such weird games, rules, regulations, and structures?" Although the rules, regulations, and structures appear arbitrary on initial examination, hidden from view is the intelligence, plan, and intent used to create them.

Players rarely question the origins of the games they play, or the apparent arbitrary nature of the rules, regulations, and structures.

They begin playing games that were invented long ago, and do exactly what they're told by "the powers that be."

The same is true of The Money Game. When examined closely and objectively, the rules, regulations, and structure of The Money Game appear arbitrary and don't make much sense either, as you'll soon see. However, in later chapters you'll see that there's a mind-blowing intelligence, plan, and intent behind the design of The Money Game, and I promise, when you find out what it is, it'll rock your world! It also opens the door to busting loose from The Money Game.

As we pass a certain age growing up, we become players in a Money Game that's already in progress. Like athletes and other game players, we never question what we're taught about playing The Money Game. We just accept the rules, regulations, and structure we're taught and play as if it was all etched in stone and absolutely nonnegotiable.

Here are three of the primary rules, regulations, and structure points we've been taught are "real" when playing The Money Game. There are actually dozens of others (including many related to taxes, governments, investing, etc.), but the following are the ones we're most familiar with and the ones that do the most damage, as you'll soon see:

1. *Limited supply.* There's a limited supply of money available to you (and/or the world) and every time money "goes out," that limited supply decreases. Therefore, you must find ways to constantly replenish your supply or you'll run out. You must also be prudent and responsible and protect your money to ensure that you don't run out of it. Because the core supply of money is limited, you must also have a long-term plan to save, invest wisely, and build assets over time to provide for your retirement years.

2. *Money moves.* There's a flow of money in and out. Money is "out there," somehow separate from you, and you must go

out to get it and bring it into your life. In addition, as you spend money, it moves away from you to others and then you have less. You have income and expenses and you must manage the movement of both so your income exceeds your expenses (profits). You must increase profits if you want to raise your quality of life.

3. *You must work harder or smarter to increase your supply of money.* You can't just have anything you want in life. Everything "costs" you. You have to "pay" for everything you want. You have to "earn" money. There is no free lunch. You don't get something for nothing. So, if you want more money, you have to find a way to add more value or work harder—or smarter—to get it. And you must develop the moneymaking skill and be totally and truly committed to making money or you'll never have much.

In support of the traditional Money Game rules, regulations, and structure, here are some common beliefs that have also been accepted as true:

- Money is the root of all evil.
- There's something dirty or bad about money—and the people who have it.
- The rich get richer and the poor get poorer.
- There's never enough.
- You must control money or it will control you.
- More money is always better.
- Money doesn't grow on trees.
- Some people have the money-making skill and others don't.
- You can't play The Money Game well *and* be spiritual.
- Net worth is the true measure of wealth and success.
- You must save for a rainy day.

It might shock you to hear me say that *none* of the rules, regulations, or beliefs I just related, and the many subset rules, regulations, and beliefs that flow from them, are true. Not one. They're all made up, as are the rules of all games. We all just accepted that they were true.

Here are two key points I'm going to plant seeds for now and then "grow tall" in Chapter 3:

1. You can't *win* The Money Game.
2. The Money Game was specifically designed to create utter and total failure.

You can't win The Money Game because:

- *There's no clear definition of winning.* How do you know if you've won The Money Game? Did you ever ask yourself that question? Do you win when you get comfortable? When you become a millionaire? A multimillionaire? A billionaire? When you surpass some other income or net worth goal you set for yourself? From my experience, while many people have financial goals they've set for themselves, few people have clear definitions of what winning The Money Game actually means. If you don't know what the target is, how can you possibly hit it or know when you've hit it?

- *Your money is always at risk.* No matter how much money you pile up, it is always at risk. You can lose all or huge chunks of it through poor management, overspending, a stock market crash, bad investments, embezzlement, theft, divorce, lawsuits, business failure, bank failure, tragic accidents, and so on. Plus, zero isn't the end. You can go way below zero into debt. The more money you have and the more intelligently you manage it, the greater the illusion of security, but the reality is, money is never truly safe, no matter how much you have or what you do with it. History is filled with stories of people who amassed enormous fortunes and then lost them (in one generation or over multiple generations).

- *There's no official ending point.* When does The Money Game end? When you reach some milestone you set for yourself? That doesn't work because even though you may temporarily reach or pass such a milestone your money is always at risk, so you could slip backward and lose what you've accumulated. When you retire? That doesn't work either. Your money is still at risk and you're still at the mercy of the other Money Game rules, regulations, and structures, even if you stop working. When you die? Well, maybe The Money Game ends for *you* at that point, but it continues for your family and heirs. If there's no official ending point for this game, how can you possibly know if or when you've won? Can you say you've won a football game if you're ahead at the end of the third quarter? Can you say you've won a baseball game if you're ahead at the end of the seventh inning? Can you say you've won an 18-hole golf tournament if you have the fewest strokes after 12 holes? No!

- *There's always a price to pay.* You also can't win The Money Game because even if you make a lot of money, keep a lot, spend a lot, manage it brilliantly, invest wisely, grow your net worth, live like a king or queen, and provide for a comfortable or even luxurious retirement, playing the game according to the traditional rules and regulations always leads to some very intense form of stress, pressure, dissatisfaction, pain, or loss— especially when it comes to free time, health, and relationships. I'm sure you've experienced this yourself, or seen or known someone who succeeded in piling up a ton of money but ended up:

—Sick

—Lonely

—Dying young

—With migraine headaches or other debilitating ailments

—An emotional basket case

—Feeling empty inside

—Living in the lap of luxury but thinking, "Is this all there is?"

- *There's always another level of success above yours.* With only a few exceptions of people at the highest levels of financial success, there's a trap built into The Money Game that most people fall into at one point or another. The trap gets sprung when someone at a specific level of financial success compares him- or herself to someone at a higher level of success and develops new desires that appear attainable but far away at that moment. For example, someone making $250,000 a year and feeling pretty good about herself sees how someone making $1 million a year lives and suddenly feels inferior by comparison. Or someone traveling first class on a commercial airline sees someone traveling by private jet, or someone with one beautiful home sees someone with two beautiful homes. Any of these can set a pattern of dissatisfaction in motion. This sort of pattern goes on and on as we move up the food chain of financial success.

Imagine playing or watching any other game with rules, regulations, and a structure like the one I just described. Imagine playing or watching a game where there's no way to know who's winning; there's no official ending point; no matter how good you get you know there's always another team or player better than you; you always end up losing (due to the price you had to pay) even if you think you're winning.

Would anyone want to play or watch a game like that? No way! For the players, it would be an absolute nightmare. No one would volunteer to play a game like that. And no one would show up to watch either. What would be the point?

Despite all of this, billions of people show up every day to play and watch The Money Game, completely oblivious to the truth about what's really going on. Many of those people believe they're winning The Money Game, believe they've won, or believe other people they see around them or in the media have won—but it's all an illusion.

In Chapter 7, I reveal an even bigger reason why you can't win The Money Game. But first I have to provide you with a few more foundational pieces of the puzzle.

What you were never told is that The Money Game is very different from the other games we play. When it comes to The Money Game, nothing is etched in stone and absolutely *everything* is negotiable. You don't need to accept the traditional rules, regulations, and structures of The Money Game. You actually have an alternative!

Since there's no way to win you have only two choices:

1. Continue to play according to the traditional rules, regulations, and structure, knowing you'll lose and pay a big price, no matter what you do.
2. Bust loose from The Money Game entirely, create a new game for yourself, choose your own rules, and transform your relationship with money *forever*.

However crazy or pie-in-the-sky it might sound to you, I guarantee that once you finish this book you'll be empowered to take the second option and bust loose from The Money Game entirely.

To continue your journey, discover three questions that have haunted you your entire life, and learn how to answer them in a way that empowers you to bust loose from The Money Game. Turn the page and continue on to Chapter 2.

The Three
Haunting Questions

Living is my job and my art.[1]
—Michel Eyquem De Montaigne,
Essayist (1533–1592)

If I could only remember that the days were not bricks to be laid row on row, to be built into a solid house, where one might dwell in safety and peace, but only food for the fires of the heart.[2]

—Edmund Wilson, Critic and
Writer (1895–1972)

Throughout recorded history, three questions have haunted humanity:

1. Who am I?
2. Why am I here?
3. What's my purpose?

As you'll soon see, even if it doesn't seem clear immediately, without practical answers to those three haunting questions, busting loose from The Money Game isn't possible. You might also find it interesting to know that many of the puzzle pieces I'll be sharing in this chapter (and the two chapters that follow) were the very pieces my grandfather shared with me over that fateful cup of hot chocolate in Crans, Switzerland. Because of the respect, even awe, I felt for my grandfather and his achievements, I accepted the concepts you're about to discover without question. However, they didn't become real for me, I didn't fully understand their significance or power, and I wasn't able to take any practical action from them until decades later—after I'd assembled more puzzle pieces and had more of the experiences I'll be sharing with you in the pages that follow.

My belief is there's no way to know the absolute Truth about the answers to those questions. Why? Because there are certain mysteries that are so huge and complex that they're beyond our understanding at our present level of consciousness and evolution. Since we can't be absolutely certain about the answers to the three haunting questions, all we can do is create models that approximate The Truth closely enough to give us practical benefit in our daily lives.

Therefore, what I'm going to share with you in the next few chapters is a working model that can truly empower you to bust loose from The Money Game. Is the model perfect? No. Can you pick holes in it if you try? Yes. What I can tell you is, despite its admitted weaknesses, it works *extremely* well. As I share the philosophical component of the model in this chapter and the next, if it seems a bit "airy-fairy" or "warm and fuzzy" to you, keep two thoughts in mind:

1. These are important puzzle pieces, no matter how they may seem at first glance. Once you reach Chapter 6, you'll understand how important they really are—and once you turn the last page of the book, your understanding of their significance will deepen further.

2. In Chapters 4 and 5, I'll be sharing the cutting-edge science that documents and validates the philosophical components of the model. That will be valuable for you if you have any

challenges believing or accepting what I share in this chapter and the next.

Let's take a look at the first haunting question.

Who Am I?

If you've had exposure to books, tapes, or seminars about what's been called new age, metaphysical, or spiritual thought, you've no doubt heard something like this: "We are spiritual beings having a physical experience." I agree with that statement, and it aligns perfectly with the model I'm presenting to you.

Who you *really are* is an infinitely powerful and magnificent being. Snap your fingers and boom, anything you want instantly manifests. No concept of power you're familiar with comes even close to the infinite power and omnipotence of who you really are. All the forces of nature and man put together and multiplied a billion times are but a speck compared to the power at your disposal. Depending on your history and the beliefs you formed living through it, this is something that may sound or feel alien to you. However, it's also one of the things you'll be able to *prove to yourself and actually experience* if you follow the guidance I offer in this book.

Because you have the power to create absolutely anything you want, your natural state is one of Infinite Abundance. In your natural state you don't "lack" anything. Nothing is missing. No desire ever goes unfulfilled. As an Infinite Being, you're also in a constant state of joyfulness and peace.

As an infinitely powerful, wise, and abundant being, you have an unlimited desire to express creatively and fully experience the expansion and joy that comes from that expression. In fact, as you'll also soon see, all of human life is essentially about creative expression, no matter what it looks like.

Now let's take a look at the second haunting question.

Why Am I Here?

You came here to play a game! In your daily life, you go about your daily routine. Then, from time to time, you step out of your routine to play games of various kinds. When I say games, I mean sports, board games, cards, mountain climbing, bike riding, bungee-jumping, driving cars at high speeds, watching TV or movies or plays, reading a great novel, painting, singing, listening to music, or whatever you really love to do. You choose to play games for fun, enjoyment, entertainment, to challenge yourself, to explore what's possible, to stretch and expand.

The same is true when it comes to why you're here. Coming from the place of being an Infinite Being, at another level of Consciousness, you decided to take time away from your daily routine to play a game, too. That game is called *The Human Game* of which *The Money Game* is a major subset.

Does this surprise you? Does playing a game seem too trivial a reason to be here or to explain what we call the pain, hardship, and complexity of human life? If so, stick with me as more and more puzzle pieces are revealed.

Let's now look at the third haunting question.

What's My Purpose?

You have a general purpose and a specific purpose. The general purpose is to play The Human Game and receive the benefits people receive from playing *all* games: fun, enjoyment, entertainment, challenge, stretching, expansion, exploration, pushing the envelope of what's possible, and so on.

Your specific purpose is to play The Human Game in the unique and precise way you choose as a unique Infinite Being. We all play The Human Game, but we do it in completely different ways. Even when it looks like we're doing the same things, doing things the same way, or for the same reasons, we're not. Everything is custom designed for us as unique Infinite Beings, as you'll clearly see after completing Chapters 4 and 5.

In *The Creating Cosmos*, Barbara Dewey said (using the term "Creating Cosmos" where I use the term "Human Game"):

> In the final analysis, I don't suppose the Creating Cosmos has a purpose greater than the joyful expression of creative possibility. Solely in the service of that purpose it is a design of the most sublime construction. It is breathtaking both in its simplicity and its opportunity. It grants total freedom within a context of cooperation and partnership. There are no winners and losers in the Creating Cosmos concept. Because each plays a game of his own choosing there are only winners.[3]

As we discussed in Chapter 1, all games start out with a concept. Then a playing field is built, then necessary tools and support resources (like golf clubs, footballs, baseballs, tennis rackets) are created, then rules, regulations, and structures are developed to which all players must strictly adhere if they want to play. It's the same with The Human Game.

Let's now discuss the concept that drives The Human Game. I'm a big fan of the *Star Trek* television and movie series. In that show, there's a concept called the "Prime Directive." The Prime Directive is a core principle that guides the actions of the crew of the Starship Enterprise as they explore space. The Human Game has a Prime Directive, too. It's to fully explore what happens when you limit unlimited power, when you limit the infinite ability to express creatively, when you limit the infinite wisdom, abundance, joyfulness, and peace that's your natural state. I'm going to introduce this concept from a philosophical perspective in this chapter and then continue the discussion from a nuts-and-bolts, day-to-day, practical perspective in Chapter 7 after a few more important puzzle pieces have been delivered to you.

All the games we play were originally invented by someone who had a specific reason and motivation for creating them. The Human Game is no exception. From an expanded and infinite perspective, imagine that one Infinite Being thought, "Wouldn't it be interesting to see what would happen if I limited myself, restricted myself, hid all my power, wisdom, abundance, and joyfulness? Could I actually convince myself it was gone? Could I actually convince myself I'm the exact opposite of who I really am? What then? What would the whole journey and experience be like if I could pull it off?"

Since you're an Infinite Being, if you want to play a game of limitation and restriction, you have to create an alternative Self or Persona to be the main player of that game. You must then hide all awareness of who you really are and all your power, wisdom, abundance, joyfulness, and peace from that Persona. You must then create other players to play The Human Game with you, a playing field on which to play, and a helper who can secretly guide you while you're blind to The Truth about who you really are and what's really going on.

The Persona who plays The Human Game is the part of you who's reading this book right now—the part you've always thought of as "you." The other players, as we'll discuss in detail in Chapter 6, are the people you see around you and interact with. The playing field is what we call the Universe or physical reality or three-dimensional reality. The helper who secretly guides you is the Real You, your Infinite Self, whom I'll be calling your *Expanded Self* throughout this book.

Words get tricky here, but it's important to understand that while the Persona and Expanded Self aspects of you feel and appear separate, they're actually one and the same Infinite Being that's unified at a very deep and profound level. The apparent separation is a necessary part of the illusion created by sleight of hand in Consciousness we'll be discussing in the next three chapters.

From the moment you, the Persona, is born, you actually begin hiding your tremendous power, wisdom, and abundance from yourself and constructing an alternative reality (playing field) on which to play The Human Game. Before we continue our discussion of limitation, restriction, and The Human Game, allow me to plant the following seed in your expanding awareness which also comes from Barbara Dewey:

> We mistakenly believe, therefore, that we are at the mercy of life rather than its creators. Such beliefs make us feel impotent and we have hastened to fill in for these perceived weaknesses with technological aids. We are not encouraged to use our natural tele-pathic capacities. We have phones. We do not need total recall. We have computers. We do not need our homing instincts. We have maps. We do not need to practice health. We have doctors.[4]

In addition to hiding your power and creating an alternative reality on which to play The Human Game, you also convince your-self the hiding places are so painful, dangerous, scary, and deadly that they should be avoided at all costs, which we'll also discuss in later chapters.

Just as a baseball game has nine innings, football games have four quarters, and golf has 18 holes, The Human Game has two phases.

Phase 1

During Phase 1 of The Human Game, your Expanded Self uses all your power, creativity, and ingenuity to hide all awareness of who you really are and what your natural state is—and to keep you from finding it at any cost. Everything possible is done to convince you that the Persona and the three-dimensional playing field are real, and to limit and restrict you more and more until you're absolutely convinced you're the exact opposite of who you really are. In the popular success and self-help literature, this process is defined very differently and is generally called "programming" or "conditioning."

As you ponder this, ask yourself if you think it's any accident that The Human Game begins with us being born as helpless infants with no power, knowledge, or abundance of any kind!

Phase 2

After forgetting who you really are and deeply immersing yourself in severely limiting and restrictive experiences in Phase 1 of The Human Game, your Expanded Self starts nudging you into Phase 2. At that point, you begin to feel incomplete, like you're missing something, like nothing makes sense any more, like there must be something else going on you don't know about. You then start looking for answers and a higher purpose for your life.

At that point, you still don't remember who you really are or how much power, wisdom, and abundance you actually possess, but you begin searching for The Truth nevertheless. Your Expanded Self then flips roles, takes you on the Treasure Hunt of the Century and supports you in reclaiming all the power, wisdom, and abundance you hid in Phase 1. Once you reclaim your power, wisdom, and abundance, you can then start playing The Human Game without limits or restrictions of any kind. I call that crossing the *Busting Loose Point* which we'll be discussing in later chapters. That's when things get very cool.

By the way, it's no accident that you found your way to this book. You wouldn't be reading my words here unless, on some level, you wanted support in jumping into Phase 2 or you're getting ready to jump into Phase 2 and are using this book as basic training or warm up.

As you've been following along with me, this thought may have crossed your mind: "Why would anyone want to play a game like that? Have so much power, abundance, and wisdom, hide it, then find it again. It sounds crazy."

If thoughts like that did cross your mind, let me ask you two questions in response:

1. Why does anybody play *any* game?
2. If you take an honest and objective look, are the rules, regulations, and structure of The Human Game really any more arbitrary or crazy than those of golf, baseball, basketball, soccer, football, chess, checkers, or Monopoly?

As we discussed earlier, people play games for the sheer fun, challenge, and exhilaration of playing, no matter how crazy they may seem at first glance or how difficult playing gets at times. People spend enormous amounts of time, energy, and money training for, playing, and watching games of all kinds and feel it's a perfectly legitimate activity. Why would it be any different for an Infinite Being with much more power, wisdom, and abundance?

Or think about this: Why would someone willingly leave their warm and comfortable home to experience pain, hardship and risk of death to participate in activities like climbing Mt. Everest or driving a high-speed racing car?

Here's the answer to all the questions like these that have occurred or may occur to you: Who you really are is a wonderfully adventurous spirit, ever eager to expand Itself and Its experiences. The Human Game of limitation is no big deal to the Real You. The real challenge of The Human Game is forgetting who you really are and hiding all your power so you can play in the first place!

Plus, consider this. Imagine you're an architect and you're hired to design an amazing building for a client. You visualize it in your imagination, then draw up the plans. That's a lot of fun and very rewarding, but it's even more exciting to see the building actually rise up in three dimensions and become "real." The challenge, fun, and reward that come from embracing The Human Game idea, then seeing it manifest in three dimensions, then actually playing it is enormous. Just let this thought incubate for a while as I offer you more and more puzzle pieces.

The following may also have occurred to you: "Okay, maybe I can buy the idea of life being a game, but why would someone willingly *choose* to experience such horrors as abuse, sickness, poverty, struggle, starvation, rape, murder, and death as part of playing? Those things don't seem particularly fun or entertaining to me."

I'll be discussing this in more detail in the chapters that follow, but for now, let me share a few thoughts: Who you really are sees no horror in any of those experiences and is actually having an absolute blast playing The Human Game. The Real You knows none of those experiences are real and it is all just a game—just like you know what's happening up on the screen in a movie isn't real. The movie may scare or exhilarate you, but you know it's all made up and no one *really* gets sick, hurt, lives, dies, or makes a million bucks.

The Real You knows all experiences in The Human Game are simply made up to create a game and a playing field on which to play. The Real You knows all your experiences only *seem real* and horrible to the Personas who are totally immersed within them and convinced they're real—and that's the whole point of The Human Game—to make it all seem real when it's not.

Making the illusion appear real was the biggest challenge in the design of The Human Game. However, beyond appearing real, The Human Game must be fascinating and hold our interest. Consider what Sol Stein, a master editor of some of the most successful writers of our century, wrote about the art of crafting truly compelling fiction:

> When the baseball, football, or basketball season is at its height, a considerable portion of the American male population and a not insignificant number of females deploy hours away from work watching their sport on television. What the baseball fan, for instance, hopes for, consciously or not, are the moments of tension and suspense when a ball is hit but not yet caught, when a runner is headed for a base and has not yet reached it. The same applies to other sports as well. The spectator rooting for his hero experiences tension, suspense, anxiety, and pleasure, all things the readers hope for when they turn to a novel. The reader is enjoying the anticipation and excitement that are often worrying in life but a pleasure when they are happening on the ball field or in a book.[5]

The same is true for us as Infinite Beings in our Human Game total immersion movie experiences. We too want to experience tension, suspense, anxiety, and pleasure through our experiences. Stein continued by saying:

> But let us remember that when a team—even the team we are rooting for—is winning too easily, our enjoyment of the game decreases. What the sports spectator and the reader enjoy most is a contest of two strong teams, a game whose outcome hangs in the balance as long as possible.[6]

Stein's wise observations also shed light on why Phase 1 life isn't perfect and why we therefore create ups and downs, challenges, and the illusion of conflict in our total immersion movie experiences.

The metaphor I'd like you to keep in mind for this going forward is the sun and clouds. Who you really are is an infinitely powerful, wise, and abundant being. Compare that to the sun. When you think about the sun, you think about enormous amounts of energy and power, right? It's a good fit.

When you play The Human Game, however, you must create illusions that convince you you're the exact opposite of who you really are—that is, convince you you're a severely limited, restricted, vulnerable, fragile, poor, and weak creature who gets tossed about by people, places, and things you have no control over. That's the equivalent of creating a bunch of clouds, putting them in front of the sun, and convincing yourself there's no sun, the clouds are real, and the clouds are all there is.

To extend the metaphor, if it's cloudy out, is the sun still shining? Yes. When there's a hurricane blowing, is the sun still shining? Yes. If it's raining, is the sun still shining? Yes. No matter what happens on our planet, the sun is always shining.

It's the same with you. No matter what's going on in your life, no matter what the circumstances look like, who you *really* are doesn't change. You're still an Infinite Being whose natural state is infinite power, abundance, wisdom, joyfulness, and peace. You just convinced yourself the opposite is true, and I explain exactly how you did that in Chapters 4 and 5.

If you start out as an Infinite Being and in Phase 1 of The Human Game the goal is to limit yourself and convince yourself you're exactly the opposite of who you really are, things can't work perfectly. You must have problems. Things can't make sense if examined closely and objectively. You've got to be uncomfortable a lot of the time. You can't experience true financial abundance, or at least not without a *huge* cost as we discussed. You can't feel consistently peaceful, satisfied, fulfilled, or happy. It's just not possible.

Blocks and resistance to achieving your goals and fulfilling your desires must be common in Phase 1. The feeling there's something missing or something wrong must nag at you, loudly or quietly. Why? Because that's the whole point of Phase 1—to convince yourself you're the exact opposite of who you really are. If the goal is to limit, you don't expand. If the goal is to restrict, you don't open up. That's the way it works.

| KEY POINT | To make Phase 1 of The Human Game work, all Truth must be distorted or skewed to keep you away from it—and your power. |

To make Phase 1 of The Human Game work, all Truth must be distorted or skewed to keep you away from it—and your power.

As we discussed, the whole goal of Phase 1 in The Human Game is to convince yourself you're the exact opposite of who you really are. Therefore, whenever any teaching attempts to explain what The Human Game is all about or how to play it in Phase 1, that teaching must be skewed or distorted or something important must be left out.

In addition, to keep you away from your power and The Truth, the techniques offered in association with that skewed and distorted Truth must be sabotaged so they don't "work"—at all or consistently. If you accept my challenge in Chapter 12 and leap through the portal into Phase 2, you'll see this everywhere—in the self-help literature, philosophy, metaphysics, mysticism, science, and religion. You'll look at what's being taught, track it, and say, "That's True, that's True, that's True, oh. . . ." And you'll see exactly where it got skewed or distorted or something was left out. It's actually quite fascinating.

For example, when studying the popular self-help technique called visualization, you're taught you have unlimited power and can create any result you want if you just see a vivid picture of the result in your mind's eye. It's true that you have unlimited power in your natural state. However, you hide that power from yourself in Phase 1 of The Human Game so it's not really available to you, the star of your movie. It's true that "You" (meaning who you really are, your Expanded Self) can create anything you want. However, that process doesn't take place in the "mind's eye" you have as the Persona and star of your movie. It takes place somewhere else, as you'll discover in Chapters 4 and 5.

The whole idea of visualization, affirmations, manifestation techniques, the Law of Attraction, and other popular self-help techniques are brilliant Phase 1 creations. Why? Because we create them, we convince ourselves they're real, we apply them, but they don't work consistently, and that creates confusion, frustration, and limitations that perfectly support the goals of Phase 1.

As I mentioned in the Introduction, I created a similar dynamic with my own *Invisible Path to Success* and *11th Element* work. I had a clear lock on a lot of The Truth but to play in Phase 1 of The Human Game, I had to skew it ever so slightly so my System would ultimately fail and keep me locked in limitation and restriction—until I was ready to enter Phase 2.

Phase 1 of The Human Game is designed to take you to the point where you feel enormous frustration and pain, where you start to feel incomplete, like something's wrong, that there must be more to life, that something else must be going on that you don't know about. Reaching that point at a very high level of intensity is the signal you're ready to move into Phase 2 (or at least expand your view of what's possible for yourself).

| KEY POINT | Part of the Phase 1 strategy involves teasing yourself into |

believing you can fix things, improve things, get things running smoothly, get everything you want, become wealthy and happy. By design, however, that can never happen while you're playing Phase 1 of The Human Game—despite what all the self-help, success, personal growth, and spiritual gurus claim. This is a subtle but very important distinction to "get."

Remember, whenever you decide to play a game—whether it's chess, checkers, football, basketball, high-speed racing, mountain climbing, or whatever, you have to play by the rules, follow the regulations, and respect the structure or you can't play.

When playing The Human Game, true power, happiness, abundance, joyfulness, and peace don't "return" until you've been playing in Phase 2 for a while, which I'm going to show you how to do. It's in Phase 2 that a gateway opens and allows you to bust loose from The Money Game. I call that gateway the *Busting Loose Point* that we'll be discussing in detail in later chapters, after I've laid a solid foundation for you.

When you're ready to discover more of The Truth about The Human Game and the true nature of the playing field we designed to play it on, turn the page to begin Chapter 3.

Leaving Hollywood in the Dust

All the world's a stage, and all the men and women merely players. They have their exits and their entrances, and one man in his time plays many parts.

—William Shakespeare, As You Like It[1]

I'd now like to introduce two additional metaphors that will support you in understanding the true nature of The Human Game, The Money Game, the field on which we play those games, and prepare you for the scientific documentation that follows in the next chapter. The metaphors revolve around amusement parks and movies.

An amusement park is a place that was specifically designed to offer rides and attractions to entertain you. You go to an amusement park by choice. Nobody drags you or forces you to go. You generally go with people you know. You experience the rides and attractions that appeal to you and ignore the ones that don't. You arrive and leave as you prefer. You go once or return multiple times. I now invite you to look at the world or what we call *three-dimensional reality* as if it were a gigantic amusement park.

If you're an Infinite Being and you're going to play a game, you can't just play *any* game. You'd be bored out of your mind. It would be like a professional basketball team playing an eighth-grade basketball team. There would be no challenge, no point, no real game. If you, as an Infinite Being, are going to play a game, it must be the ultimate game. It must be extremely sophisticated and complex and cleverly designed to keep you riveted, challenged, and on the edge of your seat at all times. That's no simple task!

Therefore, continuing the metaphor, to play The Human Game, a gigantic amusement park had to be created that would offer a wide variety of extremely complex rides and attractions (games). One of the star attractions in that amusement park is The Money Game. However, unlike familiar amusement parks such as Disney World, the amusement park in which The Human Game and The Money Game are played was designed to offer a rare breed of rides and attractions that I call *total immersion movies*.

Let's take a look at Hollywood movies for a moment. In Hollywood movies, nothing is as it appears. Every scene is carefully scripted and planned before it's filmed. Nothing ends up in the final cut of a movie unless it perfectly supports the telling of the story exactly as the creators of the movie envisioned. Nothing is random or accidental in the final cut of a movie you see on the screen. Every aspect is carefully crafted in order to have a specific impact on you—make you laugh, cry, angry, open your heart, and so on.

Everything in a Hollywood movie looks real and substantial, but it isn't. It's all made up. It's all an illusion and special effects extend the illusion to an incredible degree. You know it's an illusion as you sit in the movie theater, but you temporarily suspend your disbelief in order to be entertained. If you went behind the scenes to see how a movie is really made, what the sets actually look like, how the special effects are created and applied, what happens in the editing room, and you then looked at the final cut you saw on the screen and compared them, you'd be amazed by the complexity and the time, energy, and effort that's involved. As you know, Hollywood illusions are absolutely convincing and must be or we'd walk out of the theater or never plunk down our hard-earned money to see the movies in the first place.

All of this is true for your life and The Human Game as well. In your movie, nothing is as it appears. Every scene is carefully scripted and planned before you experience it. Nothing ends up in your movie unless it perfectly supports you in having the precise Human Game experience you want to have. Nothing is random or accidental in your movie either. Everything has been created *exactly the way it is* to support you in playing The Human Game exactly the way you want to play it, no matter how you might label or judge it at the moment. It's all carefully crafted to have a specific impact on you (especially The Money Game)—limit you and convince you you're the exact opposite of who you really are.

Just like in a Hollywood movie, everything in your world looks real and substantial, but it isn't. It's all made up. Everything you perceive with your five senses is an illusion—all props and special effects designed to create an alternative reality that allows you to play The Human Game—and your own special effects extend the illusion to an incredible degree, too. When I take you behind the scenes to show you how total immersion movies are made in The Human Game amusement park, you'll be amazed by the complexity, time, energy, and effort that's involved. It must be that way. The illusions created to support the playing of The Human Game must be absolutely convincing or The Human Game would end abruptly, the equivalent of you walking out of the theater during a boring or poorly crafted movie.

As you'll see after turning more and more pages in this book, the special effects required to make The Money Game appear real would put every special effects and animation studio in Hollywood to shame.

With Hollywood movies, millions of dollars are spent, thousands of people are involved, extremely intricate and expensive computers and other equipment are used. It sometimes takes months or even years to move from the start of a project to the moment it appears on the screen. Why is all that time, energy, effort, and money invested? "To make money," you might say. That's true, but what must happen before Hollywood can make money? You must be entertained, right? And for you to be entertained, what must happen? You must *feel* something.

Just about everyone I know loves movies. If for some reason you don't, follow along with me and you'll still get the point I want to make. Why do so many people love movies? When I ask people, most of them say:

- They're fun and entertaining.
- They provide a diversion from the daily routine.
- You can learn and grow from them.
- They enable you to see different points of view and have unique experiences.

Makes sense, doesn't it—especially in light of what we've been discussing in this chapter? However, beneath the surface of those insights is a secret few people ever uncover or fully understand. The secret is *feelings*. We love movies because of the feelings they stimulate within us. The truth is, we don't really care about the action on the screen. We just care about how the action on the screen makes us feel.

By the way, that's also why people enjoy reading books, playing and watching sports, listening to music, going to the theater, playing video games, riding roller coasters, going skydiving, climbing mountains, bungee-jumping, and so on. It's always about feelings. The external experiences only matter to the extent that they trigger inner feelings.

Think of something you really love to do—a game you love to play or watch, a task you enjoy doing, something you find extremely enjoyable. Then ask yourself, "Why do I love it so much? What's the real appeal?" You'll see that what you really love is what's going on inside of you, and what's going on outside is just the trigger.

It's the same with The Human Game. At its core, The Human Game is all about feelings and everything that happens on the screen of your total immersion movie is also just a trigger to set specific feelings into motion that support you in playing in The Human Game amusement park the way you choose to.

> | **KEY POINT** | At their core, movies, The Human Game, and The Money Game are all about *feelings*, not thinking, logic, or intellect.

Let me give you an additional illustration to deepen your understanding of this key point. I've never been a fan of baseball, but I once spoke with a friend who was fanatical about baseball. I said, "I prefer football. There's more action and a faster pace. To me, baseball is slow and boring. Why do you love it so much?"

"Baseball is primarily a mental game," he said. "The fun comes from watching the possibilities. Whenever something happens— there's a strike, a ball, an out, a bunt, a single, double, triple, or home run, whatever it is—it creates a whole new set of possibilities. Watching the possibilities and the movement of 'what would happen if . . .' scenarios is where the fun comes from."

The Human Game was designed to operate in a similar way. It too is about exploring "what would happen if . . ." scenarios because every time one thing happens, everything changes and there's a whole new set of possibilities to consider and play with. That's part of what's required to keep us interested and wanting to continue playing The Human Game.

Now, here's the really interesting part. When you're in a movie theater, you're just watching a movie. You may get very involved with the story and closely identify with the characters, but you still know you're you. You still know you're sitting in a theater watching.

You still know it's not real. You still know the action is taking place outside of you. In short, there's a distance between you and the events taking place in the movie.

When playing The Human Game in Phase 1, however, you don't just watch, you *totally immerse yourself* in the story line. Imagine sitting in a theater, seeing a movie scene start to play on the screen, stepping through the screen into the scene, forgetting who you really are and actually becoming one of the characters for a while, actually believing you're that character and everyone and everything else in the movie is real. That's what I mean by total immersion and what happens when you play The Human Game.

Let's now take a look at how a Hollywood movie is made. Then we'll bring it back to how your total-immersion Human Game movie is made. Before a Hollywood movie can be made, a subject of interest must be chosen. The movie must be *about* something. There must be a story someone wants to explore. Then, a script is written that contains the details of how the story will unfold. Then a director, cast, and crew are hired and filming starts. When the story reaches its end, filming stops.

It's the same thing with The Human Game. You have to pick specific rides or attractions in The Human Game amusement park to write stories about. I call this a mission or life purpose. What do I mean by rides and attractions? Everything you see in the physical universe and on our planet is a ride or attraction. If you're playing the role of being a parent, that's a ride in the amusement park. If you hold a job in a company, the job and company are attractions. If you teach physics in a high school, teaching and the high school are rides. As I explained earlier, The Money Game, in all its complexity and splendor, is an attraction. On and on it goes through everything you see happening in what you call "the world."

After you choose specific rides and attractions to play with, metaphorically, a script is written that details how your total immersion movie experience will unfold as you play in The Human Game amusement park. Just like in Hollywood movies, a director, in the form of your Expanded Self, is then hired to oversee your total immersion movie experience and guide and protect you on your journey. A cast is then hired, the other people playing small or large roles in The Human Game with you. Filming starts, which is the equivalent of you being born; and filming ultimately ends, which is the equivalent of you dying.

As a quick but important review, everything you see on the screen in a movie is a combination of the writer's intent, the producer's decision to make it real, the director's sensitivity to the overall purpose of the proposed project, and the various performers' abilities to support the entire effort. In other words, what you see on the screen is the final expression of a great deal of creative activity you do *not* see. Yet, it's the unseen creative activity that's the true cause and source of the story you see unfolding. It's this unseen creative activity my grandfather opened my eyes to when I was 12, the unseen creative activity I spent decades understanding and learning to fully tap, and the unseen creative activity I'll be sharing with you in the pages that follow.

When you're ready to discover The Truth about the unseen activity that creates what you experience, the unseen activity that presently keeps you locked into the limitations of The Money Game, the unseen activity that can ultimately bust you loose from The Money Game, turn the page and continue on to Chapter 4.

CHAPTER

4

The White Knight
Comes Riding In

There's no out there *out there.*[1]

—John A. Wheeler, Physicist

I dumped a lot of philosophy on you in the last two chapters. Perhaps you resonated with all of it. Maybe some of it sounded "woo-woo" to you, or you didn't see how it could relate to money or busting loose from The Money Game. As you'll soon see, the philosophy is a critical part of the Busting Loose Process, and it set us up perfectly for a discussion of the cutting edge scientific research that documents, validates, and expands the potential of the philosophy to provide practical value in your life.

Thousands of volumes have been written on the scientific research I'll be summarizing and interpreting for you here. Therefore,

I'll introduce the key concepts and then refer you to additional resources in an Appendix if you want to delve more deeply into them.

To play games, including The Human Game and The Money Game, we must have tools, support resources, and a playing field on which to play. Take baseball for example. After the inventor of the game first thought it up, he then had to physically create a diamond, bats, balls, and gloves before people could actually play the game.

The same thing is true for The Human Game. It's one thing to think or talk about creating a gigantic amusement park where total immersion movies can be created and experienced, but quite another to actually build the amusement park and make it work. So what we're going to discuss now is how our amusement park (three-dimensional reality) is created to support us in playing The Human Game.

Throughout history, people have been trying to figure out how our physical universe is structured, how it really works, and the laws that supposedly govern it. To solve such mysteries, scientists have been breaking the physical universe into smaller and smaller pieces to understand what the core building blocks are and how they interact with each other.

As scientists looked deeper and deeper, they started finding smaller and smaller particles that were given names like cells, molecules, atoms, protons, and electrons. When they penetrated more deeply into the subatomic world, however, scientists began to notice even smaller particles that didn't seem to behave according to the known laws of physics. Those discoveries led to a series of breakthroughs that are now called *quantum physics*.

When I was first introduced to quantum physics, I couldn't understand it at all. It fried my brain. It was very dense to read and wade through. But I had a sense there were important puzzle pieces for me there so I persisted. Finally, the light began to turn on, I clearly saw the puzzle pieces that were there for me, and I added them to my collection. I'm now going to share them with you.

One scientist, David Bohm, was on the forefront of the first breakthroughs in quantum physics. Bohm concluded that the only way to explain the strange behavior scientists were seeing with sub-atomic particles was that the tangible reality of our everyday lives is an illusion. Bohm asserted that underlying what we call reality was a deeper order of existence, a vast and more primary level of reality that gave birth to all the objects and appearances of our physical universe.

Michael Talbot summarized this in his book *The Holographic Universe:*

> Put another way, there is evidence to suggest that our world and everything in it—from snowflakes to maple trees to falling stars and spinning electrons—are also only ghostly images, projections from a level of reality so beyond our own it is literally beyond both space and time.[2]

Inspired by Bohm, numerous scientists kept looking for the deeper order he asserted was there. They ultimately found it in the form of a gigantic field of intelligent energy that has many names but is most often called the *Zero Point Field* (hereafter referred to as *The Field*) within the scientific community.

The Field exists as energy with infinite potential that hasn't been formed into anything yet. However, from that infinite potential, literally anything *can* be created. As scientists continued researching The Field, they developed a theory to explain how the physical universe is constructed from it. The theory involves four components:

1. The Field
2. Particles
3. The physical universe
4. Consciousness

I've already defined The Field and particles for you. You know about the physical universe. Consciousness is what physicists call *energy,* and what others have called "Mind," "Source," "Brahma," "God," and a host of other names throughout history and across cultures. It's not physical, but it's the creative force behind everything that appears in what we call the physical realm.

For the purposes of the model we're working with here, I'm going to define Consciousness as the Real You, you as an Infinite Being, which I've referred to previously as your Expanded Self. In other words: *You* are Consciousness.

Depending on the beliefs you currently hold, you may be able to accept this easily. If you have a strong belief in God or a Supreme Being, however, you may need to slightly modify this concept to say that God or a Supreme Being endowed *you* with Consciousness and power to play The Human Game. There isn't really any conflict or problem here. It just depends on how you choose to look at it. Really "getting" that *your Consciousness* is creating everything you experience is absolutely critical to busting loose from The Money Game.

Here's how the scientific theory unfolds. The Field exists in a state of infinite possibility, which means anything is possible and anything can be created from it. However, when Consciousness focuses on The Field with a specific intent to create something, that state of infinite possibility collapses into a single possibility determined by that intent. In quantum physics terms, it's called "collapsing the wave form."

Once a collapse takes place, the illusion of the physical universe is created, physical particles appear in that illusion and combine in specific ways to "build" the intended objects and living things we interact with in our daily lives—and the laws by which they appear to operate. The entire process is shaped and guided every step of the way by the original intention of the Consciousness that focused on The Field.

| KEY POINT | Dive into anything in the physical world and if you go deep enough, you end up at The Field. |

Barbara Dewey, writing in *Consciousness and Quantum Behavior*, said:

It's as if God said, "If I'm going to become physical, then I've got to carry with me all the laws which make a physical world work. I will do this by inventing a tiny particle which, through its design, will, first, create the universe and then dictate all behavior like gravity, magnetism, the strong force, and the like throughout that universe because of the way I have constructed it. At the same time—and in order to make things easier for Me—I will invent senses which make the possessors of those senses think they see and touch and hear real things, think they witness space and feel time pass, when in fact all that realness will just be an illusion."[3]

In short, scientists are documenting that you can't see anything (including money), hear anything, feel anything, experience anything (including financial ups and downs) unless *your* Consciousness creates it by focusing on The Field with a specific intent. For example, you can't see my words on this page unless *your* Consciousness focuses on The Field with the intent to create them and then actually constructs them, piece by piece, particle by particle, for you to see. This book has no independent existence or power of its own. You're the only real power and existence in the equation.

As another example, you can't see your checking account or any numbers in it unless *your* Consciousness focuses on The Field with the intent to create them and then actually constructs them, piece by piece, particle by particle, for you to see. The checking account and the numbers don't have independent existence or power of their own. You're the only power and existence in that equation, too. Does that seem hard to believe at this point? Possibly. Is it true nevertheless? Absolutely. Stick with me and you'll see for yourself.

Speaking about this phenomenon in the movie *What the Bleep Do We Know?* Amit Goswami, PhD, a brilliant scientist on the cutting edge of quantum physics and Consciousness research, said:

We all have the habit of thinking that everything around us is already a thing existing without my input, without my choice. You have to banish that kind of thinking.

Instead, you really have to recognize that even the material world around us, the chairs, the tables, the rooms, the carpet, time included, all of these are nothing but possible movements of Consciousness. And I'm choosing, moment to moment, out of those movements, to bring my actual experience into manifestation.

This is the only radical thinking that you need to do. But it is so radical, it is so difficult, because our tendency is that the world is already out there, independent of my experience.

It is not. Quantum physics has been so clear about it. Heisenberg himself, co-discoverer of quantum physics said, "Atoms are not things, they're only tendencies."

So instead of thinking of things, you have to think of possibilities. They're all possibilities of Consciousness.[4]

This concept—the observer is creating the observed and you cannot split them—is why the scientific community insists on running double-blind experiments. Why? Because scientists know if they go into an experiment with an agenda or desired outcome, they'll bias the results of the experiment. They know that by the sheer act of observing something, the observer changes it.

Barbara Dewey went on to say:

The law of cause and effect works backward for consciousness. We place cause *before* effect. We see the results building in a one-two-three process. First we have the ovum and the sperm, then the cellular division which will eventually form a fetus, and so on. We say the ovum and the sperm are the cause of all the effects which eventually lead to the birth of a baby. However, in terms of consciousness, the *idea* of a human is the *cause* of this entire process. The intermediary steps are the *effect* of the creating and causal idea of *human*. In other words, consciousness reverses cause and effect. Cause, for consciousness, is the end result. The *effect* of this cause is a physical beginning.[5]

To continue that thought, let's take the human body as an example. As scientists view it, the body is composed of subatomic particles that combine to form atoms, that combine to form molecules, that combine to form cells, that combine to form organs, that combine to form systems, that all ultimately combine to form a human body. Once assembled, each of those parts and particles has specific and very complex tasks to perform in order for the body to function. However, the true source of all of it is The Field and Consciousness.

Think about that for a minute. That's a lot of particles that must somehow be:

- Combined in specific ways
- "Glued together" once they combine into various shapes and forms so they stay in those shapes and forms
- Taught how to perform their various tasks
- Able to communicate with each other to facilitate the performance of those tasks

It is Consciousness that creates the particles from The Field, "tells" them how to combine, glues them together, teaches them how to perform their tasks, and allows them to communicate with each other as they do it.

When other games are played—such as baseball, football, soccer, volleyball, softball, or golf—you physically go to the field, court, or course to play. However, with The Human Game, you don't "go" anywhere. You're creating the whole Human Game and the entire amusement park out of *your* Consciousness, and that's where the whole Human Game is played. We're going to get more into detail on this in the chapters that follow, but for now, I want to plant that seed because it's The Truth and it's the key to busting you loose from The Money Game. Plus, the really cool thing is if you accept the invitation I extend at the end of the book, you'll have very real, very direct, and absolutely mind-blowing experiences of yourself as the Consciousness that's creating everything you experience—including money and the story of what your experience with money has been like to date.

Let's now return to the philosophy I shared in Chapters 2 and 3 and take a fresh look based on what you now know. In Chapter 3, I said who you really are is an Infinite Being with infinite power and creative ability. Do you see how that aligns perfectly with the combination of Consciousness and the infinite potential scientists attribute to The Field?

I suggested The Human Game is all about exploring "what would happen if" you limit and restrict unlimited power. Do you see how that aligns perfectly with focusing Consciousness on The Field and collapsing infinite possibility into the one possibility we call the physical universe—objects and living things—that we then explore and play with?

I suggested that to play The Human Game, we must create a playing field on which to play and then convince ourselves the playing field is real. Do you see how that aligns beautifully with the theory of how the physical universe is constructed by Consciousness? You already know how real it appears.

In the next chapter, I'll take this one step further and show you how the playing field and everything in it (including us as players) is actually created, but for now there are three key points to review and lock into your awareness.

KEY POINTS

- Consciousness creates everything you experience, down to the smallest detail (including money and every aspect of The Money Game).
- You and your Expanded Self *are* Consciousness, so *you* are creating everything you experience, down to the smallest detail (including money and every aspect of The Money Game).
- The Human Game is a game being played entirely *in* Consciousness, and every detail is custom-designed by your Expanded Self to support you in playing The Human Game the precise way you want to play it.

Find it hard to believe that *you* could be creating everything you experience? Consider your dreams at night. You lie down, close your eyes, fall asleep, and have experiences. In those dreams, your Consciousness creates entire worlds—people, places, things—and they appear absolutely real and solid, yet they're not. They're all made up, all creations of your Consciousness. The same thing is true when you have daydreams or visualize experiences in your imagination.

Think about it for a minute. When you dream, you appear to see out of the eyes of the person you are in the dream, right? Yet where are the eyes? There aren't any. Where are *you* while all of this is going on? You're *not* just inside the person you appear to be. You're actually inside absolutely everything in the dream. *You* are in all the people, in all the objects, and in all the living things you interact with. *You* are even in the very space and environment the dream appears to take place in (buildings, forest, homes, cities, etc.). It's *all* you . . . all *your* Consciousness.

Really think about that. In fact, if you have a vivid dream tonight, even if you only perceive it to be a few minutes long, observe this phenomenon. You'll see people who appear real who aren't really there. You'll see objects that appear real that aren't really there. You'll see other living things (animals, plants, trees) that appear real but aren't really there either. Again, all of it is *your* Consciousness.

Has this question buzzed through your mind once or twice yet, "What does all this have to do with money?" If so, stick with me. I promise it'll become clear very soon. Just a few more puzzle pieces and we'll get there.

To discover the nuts and bolts of how Consciousness creates the playing field for The Human Game, how those nuts and bolts hold the key to how money is *really* created, and how you can turn that key in a lock to bust yourself loose from The Money Game, turn the page to begin Chapter 5.

How Money *Really* Gets Created

Toto, I have a feeling we're not in Kansas anymore.[1]
— Dorothy in *The Wizard of Oz*

T o bust loose from The Money Game, it's important to deepen your understanding of how the playing field of The Human Game is created and how your Expanded Self (Consciousness) creates all the experiences you have as a player—including the balances in your financial accounts and the apparent flow of money in and out of your life. To do that, I want to share another metaphor with you. The metaphor is that of a hologram.

As I was struggling to understand quantum physics and how the puzzle pieces I extracted from it could be assembled into my expanding model, I noticed several references to holograms. As I dove into the research and studied the true nature of holograms, I realized it was a perfect puzzle piece.

A hologram is an image of a three-dimensional object or scene that appears to be real but isn't. Many scientists on the cutting edge of quantum physics and related research believe the hologram is the perfect metaphor to illustrate how the illusion of the physical universe is made to appear real. I agree with them. In their use of the metaphor, scientists go deeply into many facets of holograms that support their work, but in this chapter I'll only be focusing on two key facets. In the Appendix, I'll show you how to get additional information if you want it.

If you've seen what you thought was a hologram in the *Star Wars* movies, on a credit card, or in another place, you saw something that had a three-dimensional look and feel, but didn't look real. Those examples are just imitations of the true power of a real hologram. However, if you saw the movie *The Matrix* or you've seen a *Star Trek* movie or television show where the characters used the "holodeck," you've seen what's really possible with holograms. In fact, at my Busting Loose from The Money Game live events, I show video clips from *The Matrix*, *Star Trek*, and other television shows and movies to give participants a strong visual image of what's possible with holograms. You'll find a resource list of those clips in the Appendix.

In *The Holographic Universe*, Michael Talbot said:

> Physicist William Tiller, head of the Department of Materials Science at Stanford University and another supporter of the holographic idea, agrees. Tiller thinks reality is similar to the "holodeck" on the television show *Star Trek: The Next Generation*. In the series, the holodeck is an environment in which occupants can call up a holographic simulation of literally any reality they desire, a lush forest, a bustling city. They can also change each simulation in any way they want, such as cause a lamp to materialize or make an unwanted table disappear. Tiller thinks the universe is also a kind of holodeck created by the "integration" of all living things. "We've created it as a vehicle of experience, and we've created the laws that govern it," he asserts. "And when we get to the frontiers of our understanding, we can in fact shift the laws so that we're also creating the physics as we go along."[2]

To explain how juicy a metaphor the hologram is, I'm going to get technical for a minute, then bring it back to a simpler explanation. A hologram is created through a very specific process. Suppose you wanted to make a hologram of an apple. To do that, you'd first bathe the apple in the light of a laser beam. Then a second laser beam is bounced off the reflected light of the first beam and the resulting interference pattern (the area where the two laser beams commingle) is captured on film or a holographic plate, as shown in Figure 5.1.

In this case, the pattern imprinted on the film would contain very specific information about the apple—its exact red color and other details of its skin; its height, width, and depth; the size, length, location, and color of the stem; perhaps the size and location of a small dent in the skin created when someone accidentally dropped it, and so on.

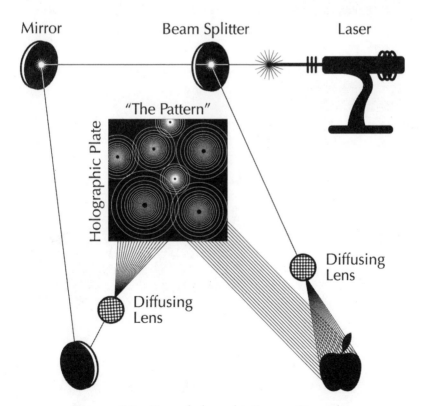

FIGURE 5.1   How a holographic "pattern" is made.

When the film is developed, it looks like a meaningless swirl of light and dark lines. But as soon as the developed film is illuminated (energized) by another laser beam, a three-dimensional image of the apple appears in space looking absolutely real and accurately depicting all the information stored in the pattern (see Figure 5.2).

With very sophisticated holograms, like in *The Matrix* or on the *Star Trek* holodeck, like engineers and scientists are currently experimenting with, and like the Hollywood special effects and animation studios are playing with, the holographic illusion is created through computers, software programs, and complex mathematical algorithms.

The two key points to focus on within the hologram metaphor are:

1. To create a hologram, which is the *illusion* of something physical, you must first create a *pattern* that holds all the details of the illusion you want to create.

2. To actually see the hologram, you must then add tremendous amounts of *power* to the pattern, which then pops out the illusion appearing to be absolutely real.

Holographic Plate

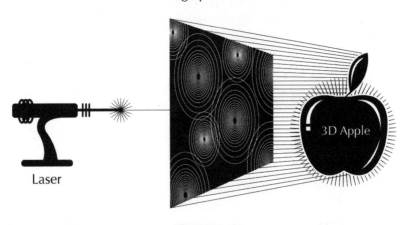

Laser

"The Pattern"

FIGURE 5.2   How an actual hologram gets created.

In other words:

Pattern + Power = Illusion

Here, then, are the components of my model for how *your Consciousness* creates the illusion of the physical universe and everything in it—and makes it appear so real that it completely fools you and allows you to play in Phase 1 of The Human Game:

- Your Consciousness approaches The Field of infinite possibility with an intention to create something and make it appear physical or real in The Human Game amusement park (a body, environment, object, animal, plant, checking account statement, cash, etc.). Your Consciousness then creates a pattern in The Field with all the necessary detail about what it wants to make physical—including all the details about you (the Persona) and all the other players of The Human Game you create to join you (body size, shape, hair color and length, personality, "aching back," and so on). Another name for these detailed patterns in popular culture is "beliefs," which we'll be discussing in detail later in the book.
- Your Consciousness then applies power (from your infinite supply) to the pattern, and the desired creation pops out as a holographic illusion.
- Because the pattern is so detailed and so much power was applied to pop it into reality, it appears absolutely real and totally convincing. This concept is illustrated in Figure 5.3.

As you move from infancy to adulthood (all just holographic creations and illusions by the way), the number of patterns in The Field (beliefs) grows exponentially to form the complex playing field you call reality and your life. Your Expanded Self controls what goes into the pattern and therefore what appears in your holographic illusion—all driven by a brilliant plan that flows out of your life purpose and mission—to perfectly support you in playing The Human Game the way that you want to play it.

FIGURE 5.3   How consciousness creates the three-dimensional world.

KEY POINT   You aren't "watching" your Human Game hologram like you'd watch a movie, play, or sporting event. Your Expanded Self is simultaneously creating the holo-gram and popping you right smack into the middle of it as the player of The Human Game.

As I mentioned earlier, Phase 1 of The Human Game is about totally immersing yourself in the illusion of the three-dimensional world and convincing yourself it's real. Your Consciousness and your Expanded Self are real. The Field is real. The patterns your Expand-ed Self creates in The Field are real. The power your Expanded Self applies to the patterns in The Field is real. But everything else you see and experience in your hologram in Phase 1 of The Human Game is just a holographic illusion. You may be able to accept this now. You may not. But if you want to bust loose from The Money Game, you must get to the point where that Truth becomes very real for you, which I'll be showing you how to do in the chapters that follow.

One of the keys to the illusion creation process is the amount of detail stored in the pattern in The Field and that's where your true power as an Infinite Being really shines through. Remember, The Human Game is designed to be an ultimate Game that tricks you into believing an illusion is real. Therefore, the amount of detail that must be stored in the patterns in The Field and the amount of power needed to pop them into your hologram is unimaginable from your current perspective.

KEY POINT If any detail in the holographic illusion misses the mark or appears fake, the illusion instantly collapses and The Human Game ends. That can't be allowed to happen, so tremendous effort is invested to make everything appear absolutely real and convincing.

Let me give you a mind-blowing illustration of this that was related to me recently. In *The Lord of The Rings* movie trilogy, there's a character named Gollum. While all the human characters in the movie were played by real people, Gollum was primarily computer generated. In making the final movie in the trilogy, *Lord of the Rings: The Return of the King*, the creators created an artificial world they wanted you to accept as real. Since Gollum was in so many scenes with other humans in that artificial world (which looked absolutely real), they didn't want him to stand out as looking fake because if he did, the illusion would be blown and your movie experience would suffer. Therefore, they needed Gollum to appear as real as the people.

Although Gollum was primarily computer generated, his movements and expressions were directly animated by an actor using a technique called *Motion Capture*. The motions of the actor were digitally recorded in three dimensions and transferred to Gollum.

Within the special effects and animation industries in Hollywood, gigantic strides have been taken with making animated people, animals, monsters, creatures, settings, and objects look real. Interestingly enough, when it comes to people, one of the most challenging features to model and animate has been hair, which, as it turns out, is a very complicated creation. It has so many layers and facets to it. It changes dramatically as people move, when it's blown by a breeze or wind, when it's wet or dry, and so on. Therefore, simulating hair realistically is an enormously complex challenge that had not yet been fully overcome by animators.

With each film Hollywood releases, most studios will invest in an aspect of computer animation to push the envelope, tell their story better, and differentiate themselves in an effort to compel audiences to see their films. Most audiences today are visually sophisticated and expect to see a new set of special effects—like hair or realistic dinosaurs, giant apes, or a superhero.

Since the special effects and animation experts made the commitment to make Gollum's hair look absolutely real (even though he didn't have much hair), they teamed up with several of the biggest movie studios and spent months and millions of dollars having brilliant programmers finally develop computer algorithms and software that could do it. Does this sound crazy or like overkill to you—all that money and effort just for hair? If so, remember what's at stake. If the illusion collapses, so does the project—and millions of dollars in profits.

The same thing is true for The Human Game and the holographic illusions you call reality. You can't see or experience anything unless your Expanded Self creates a pattern in The Field and adds power to pop it out—and whatever is in the pattern is what you see and experience (including money, bank balances, and financial statements). Like Hollywood, Consciousness is constantly pushing the envelope on making the patterns more and more sophisticated and the illusion appear more and more real.

If you look down at the floor in front of you right now and see a carpet with a stain on it, or a wooden floor with a scratch on it, they're the result of details in patterns in The Field. There's no carpet there, no stain, no wood, no scratch. It's all made up, an illusion. But the illusion must be so complex, so detailed and incredibly refined or it won't fool you, and if it doesn't fool you, if even the tiniest detail is out of place . . . "Game Over."

| KEY POINT | Actually pulling off the illusion of the playing field, the amuse-

ment park for The Human Game, and making everyone and everything appear absolutely real, is an amazing accomplishment and one of the most amazing aspects of who we really are and how much power we really have.

But it goes beyond that. If you're going to create the illusion of a human body in your hologram, that body must not only appear real, it must also provide excellent raw material for playing The Human Game. For example, you can't create the illusion of a body and have it be empty inside. There must appear to be something inside the body that people can play with and study (through biology and medicine). That's why the body was created to appear to be assembled out of subatomic particles, atoms, molecules, cells, organs, and systems. That's why the body appears to have veins, arteries, blood, other fluids, a heart, brain, and so on.

As another example, if you create an ocean in your hologram, it can't stop at the surface. You must also create a world beneath it so people can dive into it, play in it, and study it (through swimming, snorkeling, scuba diving, and oceanography). If you're going to create space in your hologram, you must create something in that space—stars, planets, comets, galaxies, and black holes—so people can look up, wonder about it, explore it, and even fly through it (astronomy and spacecraft).

If you create billions of people, they can't have just appeared out of nowhere, so you must create a storyline to explain them and make them believable, and again, to give players something to study (history, evolution, archaeology). On and on it goes for all the sciences and other creations in The Human Game amusement park.

As we discussed, in Phase 1 of The Human Game, the goal is to create patterns in The Field and pop illusions into your hologram to limit you—hide your power, wisdom, and abundance—and convince you you're the exact opposite to who you *really* are. Therefore, it should come as no surprise that so many of the experiences you've had in your life up until now—including with money—have been frustrating, annoying, difficult, and different than what you would have preferred. However, that's the way the patterns were designed, that's what power was applied to, and that's what *had* to pop into your hologram as a result.

All of us could create long lists of complaints about our lives and the holograms we find ourselves immersed in. If you thought about it, I'm sure there are many things you'd love to make go away in your life, other things you'd like to show up or increase (like your supply of money), and other things you'd like to change, tweak, or improve in various ways. As Phase 1 players, by design, we become absolute masters at harshly judging our holographic creations, which we'll be discussing in detail in Chapters 8 and 9.

However, as you now know, The Truth is we're all brilliant and amazing creators—quantum special effects animators you might say. Nothing you see in your hologram is real. It's all an illusion, all made up, all smoke and mirrors—whether you judge it good or bad or better or worse. The fact that we can make smoke and mirrors seem so real is an absolute miracle. The fact that we can actually look at an absolute miracle and judge it as bad, lousy, terrible, awful, needing change, fixing, improvement, or want to make it go away is even more of a miracle. And the fact that we can actually use our make believe creations to convince ourselves we're the exact opposite of who we really are is even more of a miracle.

You're an absolute genius at creating illusions. David Copperfield beware!

By the way, if the thought hasn't already crossed your mind, it will, so I want to address it now. Scientists have been studying the hologram. Therefore, although they think it's real, they've actually been studying the illusion. However, within the illusion, and particularly within quantum physics and related scientific fields, we left clues for ourselves to The Truth and it's those clues that I've drawn from and shared with you in this and the preceding chapter.

KEY POINTS

- You + Your Expanded Self = Consciousness
- You're not just *watching* a hologram, you're actually creating everything in it—including yourself.
- *Nothing* you experience is real.
- It's all completely made up.
- It's all a creation of *your* Consciousness.
- Your Expanded Self has direct access to The Field.
- Your Expanded Self designs the patterns.
- Your Expanded Self manages the application of power to the patterns.
- Your Expanded Self controls what pops into your holographic illusion as guided by the life purpose and mission you chose when you decided to play The Human Game.

I'd like to tie this back to money *briefly*, then we'll pick it up again in greater detail in Chapter 7. What is money? Money is a holographic illusion like everything else in The Human Game. Where does money come from? Your Consciousness, like everything else in The Human Game. Money does *not* come from anyone or anything in the hologram, even though it appears to and you've convinced yourself it does. Whatever your current or past financial situation, whatever amount of money appears to be in your accounts right now, whatever debt you appear to have, whatever your income and net worth appear to be, it was all created by the combination of patterns in The Field *you* put there and the tremendous power *you* applied to pop the illusion of them into your hologram.

As far out as this may sound *at this point*, it's actually what opens the door to busting you loose from The Money Game. Why? Because as you'll soon see, in Phase 2 of The Human Game, you have the opportunity to reclaim the power that was applied to the limiting financial patterns in The Field in Phase 1, collapse those patterns, and once again experience the Infinite Abundance that's your natural state. This is very real and very doable, and I'll be showing you how to do it, simple step by simple step, as we continue our journey together.

As we conclude this chapter, please remember what I said in the Introduction: that you don't need to take my word on anything I just shared with you, whether it makes logical sense and "feels right" to you or not. If you accept my invitation in Chapter 15 and make the leap into Phase 2, you'll have experiences that will prove to you, beyond the shadow of any doubt, that everything I just shared is true.

I don't know what those experiences will look like for you since everything in your Human Game is customized for you. It could be anything, whatever it takes to get you where you want to go—in the way you want to get there. But it will consist of some really "weird" stuff like you going into a store, buying a blue shirt, seeing the clerk put the blue shirt into your bag, getting home, opening the bag and seeing a pink shirt inside. Since there isn't any blue shirt, just the illusion of one created from a pattern in The Field, it's no big deal for your Expanded Self to change the pattern to say "the shirt is pink." I've had many experiences like that as have my clients. I'll be sharing many stories to illustrate what can happen in Phase 2 in Chapter 12.

To discover who all the other people in your hologram *really* are and how they *really* interact with you to support you in playing The Human Game, turn the page to begin Chapter 6 and continue your journey into busting loose from The Money Game.

Mirror, Mirror on the Wall

We cannot, each of us, be the butcher, the baker, and the candlestick maker, but if you are the baker and I am the butcher we can live within the spectrum of possibility.[1]

—Barbara Dewey

A human being is a part of a whole, called by us "universe," a part limited in time and space. He experiences himself, his thoughts and feelings as something separated from the rest . . . a kind of optical delusion of his consciousness.[2]

—Albert Einstein

There are some games we prefer to play alone. But most games are played with other players. The same is true of The Human Game. If you created an elaborate playing field for a game and no one else was there to play with you, it wouldn't be much fun or do you much good, would it? Plus, going back to what we discussed in the previous chapter, the illusion wouldn't be very believable if you were the only living thing in your entire amusement park.

Therefore, as part of playing The Human Game, you create other players in your hologram so it will appear real, to assist you in playing, and to allow for the kind of complexity that's needed to keep your challenge, interest, and enjoyment levels high. Just like in a dream, these "other people" aren't actually separate from you. They're part of *you*, other aspects of *you*, creations of *your* Consciousness. That's why I call this chapter "Mirror, Mirror on the Wall."

You can compare the role other people play in your hologram to the role actors play in Hollywood movies. Hollywood actors appear in movies by choice and agreement. They enter and exit the stage when they're told to. If they agree to play a particular role, they're given a script that gives them specific lines to say and actions to take, and they say and do what they're told.

In a Hollywood movie, there are actors who play large parts we call starring roles. Others play smaller parts we call supporting roles. Others play tiny parts we call cameos. Still other actors who remain in the background and never speak or have impact on the central characters are called extras. Extras are just there to make the scenes appear real.

The same thing is true for your Human Game holographic total immersion movie experience, and interestingly enough, most of the people you "see" in the world are extras or only making cameo appearances. If you really think about it, even though it looks like there are billions of people in The Human Game amusement park, only a small number of them actually interact with you and have any impact.

| KEY POINT | As hard as it may be to believe, when other players appear in *your* hologram, they're 100 percent *your* creation. No one has any power or independent decision-making authority *in your hologram* beyond what |

**your Expanded Self gives them through their
"scripts" to support you on your Human Game
journey.**

Here's a question and comment I hear often at this point in laying out the Busting Loose from The Money Game model: "You're saying my spouse, kids, parents, sister, friends, brother, and boss aren't real? They're just holographic illusions? No way. I can't accept that and I don't like how it devalues them in my mind."

If thoughts like that crossed your mind, let me share the following for now and then we'll come back to the discussion later. First, it's not just other people who aren't real. Nothing in your hologram is real as I previously defined the term for you—including you and me. We're all just part of a holographic illusion created by Consciousness to allow us to play The Human Game.

Second, as I explained in the previous chapter and as we'll delve more deeply into in Chapters 8 and 9, the entire Human Game is a miracle, an amazing accomplishment, a brilliant creation to be in absolute awe of at every moment. There's not the slightest trace of devaluing anyone or anything in my model. Quite the opposite.

Third, if you choose to play the Phase 2 game and take the action steps I share in the final chapters of the book, I absolutely guarantee, beyond the shadow of any doubt, you'll prove the validity of these concepts to yourself through the Phase 2 experiences you'll create *with the other players* you create as you play The Human Game.

When I share these concepts, it's also quite natural to wonder how I could be creating you and you could be creating me simultaneously, or how you could be creating your spouse and he or she could be creating you simultaneously, or wonder the same thing about your kids, boss, parents, brothers, sisters, friends, and so on. I must now make one key point very clear before we continue. There's a concept in quantum physics called *tangled hierarchy*. What it means, as I choose to interpret it, is if you try to resolve certain riddles from a logical or analytical perspective, it results in an endless loop that gets you nowhere.

se I say to you, "All writers are liars." Am I
...g? Try to resolve it logically. You can't. If I
...iars and I'm a writer, then I must be lying. So if
...n the opposite must be true—all writers must tell the
...ut then I'm lying when I say all writers are liars. So writers
...n't all tell the truth because they can lie, and on and on it goes in an endless loop. The only way out of the loop is to jump out of it completely.

The same thing is true of trying to figure out what's going on in someone else's hologram or what role you play in someone else's hologram. You can't do it. Trying to figure this out also creates an endless loop that gets you nowhere. For the purposes of the model I'm sharing here, and to support yourself in busting loose from The Money Game, you must keep the focus on yourself at all times. It's *your* hologram, *your* total immersion experience, *your* Game in the three-dimensional amusement park, a creation of *your* Consciousness.

Let me repeat a critical point to make sure we're on the same page: Everyone else in your hologram is an actor who says and does what you ask him or her to say and do. In your hologram, others have absolutely no power, independent existence, or independent decision-making authority. In your hologram, they're 100 percent *your* creation, and that's all you concern yourself with. You leave *their* holograms alone. If you'd like to learn a bit more about this, I have a special gift for you—an audio recording of a brief lecture I gave on the subject. Just visit this page on my web site to hear or download it: http://www.bustingloose.com/thedream.html.

By the way, a corollary of this is that you're always absolutely safe and protected in your hologram. No one else can intrude into your hologram and hurt or damage you (or anyone you care about) in any way. The only way someone could *appear* to hurt or damage you is if you create a pattern with those details in The Field, energize it, pop it into your hologram, and convince yourself it's real. And the only reason you'd do that is if having such an experience would provide perfect support for you in playing The Human Game—no matter how you might judge it from your limited Phase 1 perspective as the Persona and star of your total immersion movie.

| KEY POINT | There's no power outside of you in *your* hologram—not in |

anyone, not in anything. YOU have all the power in *your* hologram.

Everyone else who appears in your hologram was created from a pattern in The Field that was put there and energized by your Expanded Self. Remember, you can't see or experience *anything* in your hologram that isn't created *by you* in that way. All the patterns in The Field relating to other people are created to allow them to play one or more of these three roles in your hologram:

1. To reflect something back you're thinking or feeling about yourself or a belief you have
2. To share supportive knowledge, wisdom, or insight with you
3. To set something in motion to support you on your journey

We now look at each of these three possibilities separately.

Reflection

In her book *As You Believe*, Barbara Dewey wrote:

> The illusion of separation not only symbolizes our self-doubt and alienation, it gives us a chance to work through the interior distress of various dichotomies by externalizing them. We see ourselves in others, hating in them what we hate in ourselves, loving in them what we love in ourselves. We contend with others because we are contending within ourselves. We punish and reward others as we would ourselves. The illusion of separation offers us the chance to resolve the interior inhibitions to unqualified love

in a state of true union. Without this illusion and our reactions to other people, we might never even know such stresses existed.[3]

Note Dewey's use of such words as self-doubt, alienation, distress, hate, punish, and inhibitions. Do you see how beautifully it all ties into the goal of Phase 1 which is to create the illusion of limitation and restriction and convince ourselves we're the exact opposite of who we really are?

As Barbara expressed so beautifully in the preceding quote, you pop many people into your hologram to reflect back what you're thinking or feeling about yourself to support you on your journey (which takes on added significance in Phase 2 of The Human Game as we'll discuss in later chapters) or to display a belief you have about the illusion. For example, if you have a belief that you must take vitamins and exercise frequently to stay healthy, you'll pop people into your hologram who take vitamins and exercise frequently to reflect that belief back to you.

If you believe in the germ theory, that illness can pass from one person to another, that you can "catch" a cold or the flu, you'll pop people into your hologram who appear sick so you or a family member will appear to catch it from them to reflect that belief back to you. This is a particularly prevalent belief and reflection when you have kids who go to school.

If you believe that "I'm always underappreciated and underpaid at work," or "friends and family borrow money from me and never pay it back," or "people will take every opportunity to overcharge and rip you off," you'll create actors to pop into your hologram and appear to prove and provide evidence that those beliefs are all real.

As another example, if you create people who come into your hologram and treat you shabbily or ignore you (like I did when I was younger and deeply immersed in Phase 1), it's a reflection of the fact that you're treating yourself shabbily and ignoring yourself—in one way or another.

At a time when I was angry at the world and lashing out at everyone around me, I created a dog in my hologram who barked with such intensity at other people and noises I thought she'd rupture a kidney or have a heart attack. When I moved through that phase she suddenly passed away.

On and on it goes. From my experience in the laboratory of my own life and working with clients worldwide, reflections can become quite detailed and complex, just like the very nature of The Human Game. We'll discuss them in more detail in later chapters.

Knowledge, Wisdom, and Insight

To play The Human Game, there are times where it's supportive to give yourself specific nuggets of knowledge, wisdom, and insight. As a result, you'll pop teachers, speakers, experts, friends, associates, and complete strangers into your hologram to enlighten you directly—or enlighten yourself indirectly through books, magazines, newspapers, audiotapes, or videotapes you create.

As an Infinite Being, you have instant access to all knowledge, wisdom, and insight, but while playing The Human Game, you can create knowledge, wisdom, and insight *appearing* to flow to you from others by simply creating patterns in The Field, energizing them, and popping them into your hologram—just as you did with this book.

Setting Things into Motion

In Chapter 2, I gave the example of baseball and explained how The Human Game was designed to allow you to explore "what would happen if" scenarios so you could have fun tracking the possibilities and watching how everything moves when the variables change.

As a result, you frequently create people and pop them into your hologram to set things in motion to support you in playing The Human Game the way you want to play it. For example, you might create someone to pop into your hologram and offer you a job, fire you from a job, give you a lucrative contract for your business, introduce you to an influential contact, give you an investment tip, loan you money, say or do something to offend or upset you, give you a speeding ticket, or run a red light and crash into your car. In each case, such creations open doors, nudge you through them, and set powerful events in motion in your total immersion movie experience that support you perfectly in playing The Human Game exactly as you want to play it.

If you accept the invitation at the end of this book and choose to play the Phase 2 game, you'll create many people popping into your hologram to say and do things that support you in reclaiming power from the limited Phase 1 patterns in The Field, collapsing them, and appearing to assist you in busting loose from The Money Game. That's what you created me to support you in doing.

You've now completed what I call the foundational segment of the book and you're almost ready to move into the practical segment. Before doing that, however, we need to take another look at The Money Game from your now substantially expanded perspective. To do that, please turn the page and continue on to Chapter 7.

7

Turning on Your X-Ray Vision

Nobody can conceive or imagine all the wonders there are unseen and unseeable in the world.[1]

—Francis P. Church, Editor, in his *New York Sun* editorial responding to Virginia O'Hanlon's question: Is There a Santa Claus? (1839–1906)

Only he who can see the invisible can do the impossible.[2]

—Frank Gaines

I grew up reading Superman comics where the Superman character had X-ray vision. It enabled him to see what was hidden from view, what others couldn't see. Now that you understand The Human Game, The Field, Consciousness, holograms, and the Mechanics of Manifestation, you have access to your own form of X-ray vision. You now have the ability to see what's hidden from view and what others can't see. It's now time to fully awaken and enhance that skill by using it. If you stay with me, then accept my invitation and make the quantum leap into Phase 2, your X-ray vision will get stronger and stronger and more and more penetrating as you use it.

However, I must warn you that seeing The Money Game with X-ray vision is going to seriously mess with your head. This is one of the times I mentioned in the Introduction where you might feel disoriented, angry, or like you've been hit in the face with a two-by-four. You might also be tempted to think:

- "Is he crazy?"
- "He can't be serious!"
- "This isn't what I expected when I bought this book!"
- "No way!"
- "Bullshit!"

That's to be expected. I have to blow your circuits before I can replace them with new circuits that allow you to run a new kind of power through your life. Get ready for a major challenge to your status quo and know it's absolutely necessary if you want to open the portal to the new world that makes busting loose from The Money Game possible.

Also, please note that from this point forward in the book, to support you in using your X-ray vision and remind you of where Phase 1 limits, restrictions, and illusions are hiding, I'll be emphasizing certain words by putting them in italics.

The Money Game was an absolutely brilliant creation—a stroke of true genius. It was created as one of the cornerstones in Phase 1 of The Human Game. It was created specifically to limit and restrict you. It's important for you to fully appreciate just how brilliant a creation it was, so let's review the core rules and regulations of The Money Game using your X-ray vision. In Chapter 1, we discussed the three primary rules of The Money Game:

1. There's a limited supply of money available to you and/or the world.

2. Money *moves*.

3. You must add more value or work harder or smarter to increase your supply of money.

Let's take a fresh look at each of the three rules individually.

There's a Limited Supply of Money Available to You and/or the World

Based on what you now know, is that true?

No!

Where does money come from? A pattern in The Field with specific details in it. If the details specify a larger or smaller amount of money for an individual, business, state, or country, that's what will be seen and experienced in the hologram. If the details change, what's seen and experienced will change, too.

Is there any limit to the number of patterns you can insert into The Field or what details can be included in them?

No!

Is there any limit to the amount of power you can apply to pop those patterns into your hologram appearing to be real?

No!

What's the logical conclusion to draw, then? The supply of money available to you and the world is actually unlimited.

Money Moves

Here are several points that summarize the specifics of this rule:

- There's an in and out flow of money in your life.
- Money is *out there* and you must go get it and bring it into your life.

- As you spend money, it moves from you to others; you have less and they have more.
- You have income and expenses and you must make sure your income exceeds your expenses (profits).
- If you want to raise your quality of life, you must raise your *profits*.

Let's now turn on your X-ray vision again. If the real source of money is your Consciousness and The Field, not the hologram, does money actually flow or move or go anywhere at all?

No!

You've created the illusion of money moving in your hologram, but it's not real. You just convinced yourself the movement was real.

Is there any "out there" to which you can go to "get" money and bring it into your life?

No!

The Human Game is a game created by and played entirely in Consciousness.

When you spend money, do you really have less, and does another person, company, or entity really have more?

No!

All that really happened is a few details in a pattern in The Field change.

Is *income* real? Are *expenses* real? Are *profits* real? Do you really need to increase *profits* if you want to improve your quality of life?

No to all four questions!

Nothing I just described relating to rule number two in The Money Game is real. All you can do is create the illusion of movement, gain, and loss and convince yourself it's real (which you did a fantastic job of).

By the way, does money really "move" in a movie? If someone in a movie makes or loses a million dollars, earns a salary of $150,000 a year, wins the lottery, or receives an inheritance, did it really happen? Nope. It's all an illusion, just like the illusion of money moving in your hologram.

You Must Add More Value or *Work* Harder or Smarter to Increase Your Money Supply

Here are several points that summarize the specifics of this rule:

- You can't just have anything you want in life.
- Everything *costs* you.
- You have to *pay* for it.
- You have to *work* for it.
- You have to *earn* it.
- Making money is a skill some people have and others don't, and you must master it or you'll never have much money.
- There's no free lunch.
- You don't get something for nothing.

If the illusion of money comes from a pattern in The Field and you have the power to create any pattern, apply power to any pattern, and pop any pattern into your hologram appearing to be real, can you *have* anything you want?

Absolutely! You can have anything you want. The only limits are self-imposed and are created to align your experience with your mission and life purpose.

If everything you see around you—everything you could *buy, rent, lease, or own*—is just a holographic illusion created by *you*, from a pattern you put in The Field, and your power, does anything really *cost* you? Do you really have to *pay* for it, add more *value* to receive it, *work* for it (whether smartly or dumbly) or *earn* it?

No!

You can create the illusion of having to, but that's all it is. Smoke and mirrors. It is all an illusion.

Since all money comes from you and a pattern in The Field, and since the illusion of how it appears to move or show up in your hologram comes from the details in the pattern, is there any sort of money-making skill some people have, others don't, and which you must master?

No!

You can create the illusion of needing to master specific money-making skills to *make money*—like real estate, stock trading, or business building—or you can choose to master such a skill for the fun of it, but is it a rule or a must?

No, no, no!

In Chapter 1, I shared the following common beliefs about money and The Money Game that flow from the three primary rules we just reviewed:

- "Money is the root of all evil."
- "There's something dirty or bad about money—and the people who have it."
- "The rich get richer and the poor get poorer."
- "There's never enough."
- "You must control money or it will control you."
- "More money is always better."
- "Money doesn't grow on trees."
- "You can't play The Money Game well *and* be spiritual."
- "Net worth is the true measure of wealth and success."
- "You must save for a rainy day."

From what you now know, is even one of those beliefs true? Is any one even close to The Truth of how things really work?

No!

I could go on and on here, but for now, let me just ask you this: Do you see how beautifully and brilliantly the three primary rules and common beliefs that flow from them limit, restrict, and devalue you? Do you see how alien they are to The Truth of who you *really* are? Do you see how alien they are to The Truth of how things *really* work? Do you see how brilliant this was as a strategy to support the goal of Phase 1 in The Human Game—which is to convince yourself you're limited and the exact opposite of who you really are?

| KEY POINT | *Everything* in Phase 2 is the exact opposite of the way it is in Phase 1. |

By the way, in answering the questions I just posed, if you're not absolutely convinced about the philosophy I shared with you in previous chapters, consider them from the perspective of the science alone. If you consider the questions from the perspective of quantum physics alone, you still see that the fundamental rules, regulations, and structure of The Money Game go directly against The Truth of how things really work.

The Truth is, there *is* free lunch. You *can* get something for nothing. You *don't* have to add more value or work harder or smarter to increase your money supply. You *don't* have to climb any ladder to make more money.

Remember, expenses don't exist. Income doesn't exist. Profits don't exist. Bills, invoices, accounts receivable, accounts payable don't exist. They're all just holographic illusions created by your Expanded Self from patterns in The Field. Your checkbook and other financial accounts don't exist. The numbers in those accounts don't exist. The story of how the money got into those accounts isn't real. They're all just holographic illusions.

KEY POINTS

- **Money doesn't come from the hologram. It comes from *you* and The Field.**
- **There's no power in the hologram. It all comes from you.**
- **Numbers were created specifically to give you an experience of limitation and that's their real purpose.**

Because of this, the supply of money available to you is infinite. You can't "run out." You can't "lose it." You don't have to do anything to create money or increase its flow to you (although you can if playing that way would be fun for you). Prudent management is not required. Why? Because there's nothing "there" that needs managing (although you can create something and manage it if playing that way would be fun for you).

Debt doesn't exist. The concept is completely made up—as is net worth. There aren't any assets that need managing or protecting. As the Creator of everything in your hologram, when you spend, you're actually paying yourself since the money doesn't actually go anywhere else. Your supply of money does *not* decrease as you spend. It actually increases if done in alignment with Phase 2 (as you'll see in Chapter 9). When anything else appears to be true, it's a holographic illusion you've accepted as real.

KEY POINT   Abundance Just Is!

Abundance is who you really are. It's your natural state. Remember what the quantum physicists say:

The Field = Unlimited power and infinite possibility

Money is *easily* created—in *any amount* and appearing to come from *any source*—by simply creating a pattern in The Field, energizing it, and popping it into your hologram. Rich, poor, struggle, and ease are all *equal holographic creations* from different patterns in The Field. It takes the same amount of power and effort to create all of them.

KEY POINT   It takes the same amount of power and effort to create *any* illusion in the hologram—no matter how you choose to judge, label, or describe it.

Plus, consider the following which we'll discuss in more detail in Chapter 10:

- More money in your hologram isn't good.
- Less money in your hologram isn't bad.
- The amount you have was designed—at every moment—to perfectly support you in playing The Human Game the exact way you wanted to play.

Here's the bottom line: You already have all the money and "stuff" you could ever want or need.

It's already yours!

In truth, you have the power and ability to create any amount of money in your hologram appearing to flow to you or *show up* in any way. The limitations you experienced in the past and the restrictions you're experiencing now were created from limited patterns your Expanded Self created in The Field. That's it. It says nothing about who you really are and what you're really capable of except the degree to which you've been able to fool yourself.

The amazingly cool thing is you can:

- Reclaim your power from those limiting patterns and collapse them.
- Claim your Infinite Abundance and open fully into it.
- Bust loose from The Money Game—completely and permanently.

I'll be showing you how to do that in the chapters that follow!

In Chapter 1, I explained that you can't "win" The Money Game. Before we continue, let's take a fresh look at that idea using your X-ray vision. As you now know, The Real You started in the fullness of Infinite Abundance which is your natural state. The Money Game was created to give you the exact opposite experience—an experience of limitation, restriction, and finite-ness. Therefore, as long as you continue playing The Money Game from a Phase 1 perspective, you *must* continue to experience limitation and restriction in some way, shape, or form.

Plus, and listen closely here, no matter how much money you *appear* to pile up in the hologram, it's not real. It's a holographic illusion. It's still severely limited in comparison to how much you really "have," it's still fragile and vulnerable to attack and loss, and there will still be a price to pay for you as a player of The Money Game. So, what do you really want:

1. An artificial state of abundance that's fragile and designed to limit and restrict you—no matter how big the numbers appear to get?

2. Your natural state of Infinite Abundance—and an unlimited supply of money and freedom?

I chose option 2 and made the commitment to do whatever it took to become fully open to who I really am and my natural state of Infinite Abundance. That's what ultimately led me to bust loose from The Money Game.

You're now ready to discover the practical nuts-and-bolts steps for actually busting loose from The Money Game. To make that leap, turn the page and begin Chapter 8.

The Treasure Hunt
of the Century

*There is a giant asleep within every man. When the giant
awakes, miracles happen*[1]

— Frederick Faust (1892–1944)

You may have been surprised when I said in the previous chapter that you already have all the money and "stuff" you could ever want, that you can reclaim your power from the limiting patterns in The Field and fully open up into the Infinite Abundance that's your natural state. It's all true, however, and in the next two chapters I'm going to show you exactly *how* to do it.

It all begins with a simple shift in focus. In the model I've shared with you, there are three components (Figure 8.1) to everything you experience as you play The Human Game:

FIGURE 8.1 The three spheres of creation.

1. The Creator (Consciousness = Your Expanded Self)
2. The Creative Process (Patterns and power in The Field)
3. The Creations (everything you see and experience in your hologram: people, places, things, your body, and so on)

By design, until now, if you're like I was and like most people I speak with, you've focused primarily on your creations. You convinced yourself they were real, you gave your power to them, and they acted as if they were real and had power as a result. You never saw *your* Consciousness as the Creator of *everything* you experience, and you ignored the Creative Process.

If you've studied manifestation techniques, the Law of Attraction, or the metaphysical idea that you create your own reality, you may feel tempted to disagree with me. However, as I explained in Chapter 2, those teachings and techniques are Phase 1 teachings and techniques that, by necessity, had to be skewed, distorted, incomplete, or sabotaged to keep you limited and away from your power. You are now working with Phase 2 teachings that have no such limitations.

To bust loose from The Money Game, you must first shift your focus away from your Creations and onto the Creative Process and yourself as the Creator *within the context of the model in Figure 8.1*. When you do that, you can reclaim your power and fully open to the Infinite Abundance that's your natural state.

Let's review your role as the Creator of everything you experience as you play The Human Game. You're an infinitely powerful being. Your natural state is one of Infinite Abundance, infinite joy, unconditional love, and infinite appreciation for everyone and everything you create and experience. When you experience *anything else*, you know:

- Your Expanded Self created it by applying tremendous power to a pattern in The Field.
- It is a holographic illusion.
- You can reclaim the power from the illusion and collapse it.

How You Reclaim Power

To explain how you reclaim power, I use the metaphor of an Easter egg hunt. My friends Nicol and Trip Davis hold an Easter egg hunt every year. They invite dozens of children from our town to participate. They hide hundreds of plastic eggs on their property that have toys and candy inside them. When the children get the green light to start the hunt, they joyously run off to look for the eggs. When they find one, they open it, remove the candy or toy, and are absolutely delighted at their good fortune. Then they put the goodie aside and continue the hunt.

It works the same way for reclaiming power from the limiting patterns you installed in The Field in Phase 1 of The Human Game.

In Phase 2 of The Human Game, your Expanded Self takes you on a special kind of Easter egg hunt that I call *The Treasure Hunt of the Century* to find the eggs (the patterns) in The Field where you invested the greatest amount of power to limit and restrict yourself in Phase 1. You then open up those eggs, reclaim the power from them (like the children removing the candy or toys), the patterns inside those eggs collapse, and so does the limitation and restriction you were experiencing in your hologram. That's what ultimately opens you up to your natural state of Infinite Abundance.

| KEY POINT | **You don't have to "create" financial abundance. It's already there. It always was. You just hid it from yourself. In Phase 2, you simply rediscover and open into it.** |

In Chapter 2, I introduced the metaphor of the sun and clouds. I explained that who you really are is an infinitely powerful, infinitely wise, and infinitely abundant being whom I compared to the sun. Then you created a complex set of illusions and convinced yourself you were the exact opposite of who you really are. I compared those illusions to creating clouds, putting them in front of the sun and convincing yourself there's no sun, the clouds are real, and the clouds are all there is. In Phase 2, you just remove the clouds, and the sun of who you really are—the sun that was always shining anyway—shines through into your experience, naturally.

To understand how to extract power from the eggs and remove the clouds, let's take a closer look at how the eggs in The Field are created. You must understand exactly what's inside the eggs in The Field before you can fully reclaim power from them and bust loose from The Money Game. I'm going to explain what's inside the eggs in this chapter, but the explanation won't reach full significance until we discuss how to live day-to-day in Phase 2 of The Human Game in later chapters.

In Chapter 5, we discussed Hollywood movies, special effects, and the commitment of Hollywood filmmakers to make their illusions appear as real and convincing as possible—no matter how sophisticated their tricks must be to do it. We also discussed that the patterns in The Field from which the illusion of The Human Game rises must be extremely complex and absolutely convincing as well or the Game ends. The complex patterns we create in The Field are built on a foundation of what the popular self-help and psychological literature calls "beliefs." A belief is an idea or concept we make up and accept as true. The Money Game, as you've seen, is a giant collection of beliefs we made up and then invested enormous amounts of power convincing ourselves they were true.

However, just accepting an idea or concept as true and creating a belief about it isn't enough to make it appear absolutely real and *persist* in your hologram. For example, suppose you create a pattern in The Field and energize it to create the illusion of a checking account with $500 in it and bills totaling $750. "I have $500 in my checking account and $750 in bills" is therefore a belief you create. However, that belief alone doesn't have much stability or staying power. You could easily forget about the account or the $500 in it or the $750 in bills or you could forget to track how the numbers change over time. Therefore, you can't just create a pattern in The Field, put some power in it, pop it into your hologram, and expect the illusion to fool you and remain in place. You have to reinforce

ep the power in it and keep the holographic illu-
o regenerate itself. Judgment does this. Judgment is
ks" beliefs inside your hologram.

example, let's say you create a belief that you have a checking account with $500 in it and that you have $750 in bills. Let's say you then go beyond just having that belief and say to yourself, "I can't pay my bills. That's bad. I don't like that." What are you *really* saying when you judge it that way?

It's real.

When you judge a creation as being negative by saying "I don't like it" or "That's bad" or "I want that to go away" or "I want to change that" or in some cases, even if you judge it as being positive by saying "I like that" or "I want more of that" or however else you judge and describe the experience, you reinforce the illusion that it's real, you keep your power in it (or add more to it), and it stays in your hologram. At this point in the creation of an egg, the pattern in The Field now has in it details about the belief and judgment about the belief. On your travels through Phase 1 of The Human Game, I'm sure you've heard something said about judgment being unhealthy in some way, shape, or form. That's correct, but as you now know, not for the reasons you were told.

However, judgment isn't always enough to keep an illusion locked into your hologram either. Why? Because in many cases, the judgment is weak and doesn't have enough "glue" in it. Therefore, you must create "consequences" to strengthen the glue and further reinforce the pattern in The Field. Continuing with the example of a checking account and bills, what happens if you pay a bill late? You get charged *late fees*. What happens if you don't pay a bill at all? Your account gets sent to a *collection agency*. What happens if you *bounce* a check? The bank charges an *insufficient funds fee*, and if you do it enough, the bank will close your account and terminate its relationship with you which would be really *bad*.

Let's take a look at the "positive" side of this scenario. Suppose you create a belief that you have a checking account with $50,000 in it. You look at that account and judge it by saying "That's good.

I like that." The consequence you then create is feeling prosperous and having the freedom to buy or do many things that please you.

By applying your X-ray vision to these scenarios, what's the true significance of the consequences? They add more detail to the patterns in The Field and further reinforce the illusion that checking accounts, bills, creditors, banks, collection agencies, and things you can buy or do are real. It's kind of like going the extra mile to make Gollum's hair and movements appear absolutely real in *The Lord of the Rings!* Do you see how tricky, brilliant, and effective this whole process is?

Here are some of the other "negative" consequences we install within our eggs/patterns in The Field to make illusions appear even more real:

- Imprisonment
- "Time outs" for young kids or being "grounded" for teens
- Being expelled from school
- Loss of prestige or status
- Injury
- Death

Here are some "positive" consequences we install within our eggs/patterns in The Field to make illusions appear even more real:

- Financial rewards
- Feelings of pride or self-confidence
- Job promotions
- Popularity
- Efficiency and productivity
- Fame

Since you create your own playing field, rules, and regulations as you play The Human Game, you also create your own consequences—*rewards and punishments*—to enhance the illusions you create. You then punish and reward yourself by putting those rewards and punishments into patterns in The Field and adding power to them.

Figure 8.2 shows the process of creating an egg that creates recurring illusions in your hologram which appear absolutely real.

Creating beliefs, judging them, adding consequences, then applying tremendous power to make the now enhanced pattern pop into your hologram and appear unquestionably real is the creative cycle that locks you into limitation and restriction in Phase 1 of The Human Game—and it applies to absolutely everything you see and experience in your hologram. The other interesting thing to note is that once an enhanced pattern is created in this way, and the experience recurs in your hologram, each successive time you look at it you say to yourself, "You see, it is real!" and the apparent evidence of its reality locks it even more deeply into your hologram.

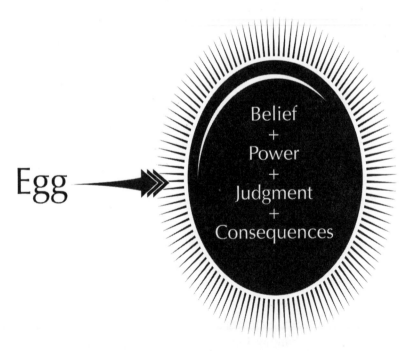

FIGURE 8.2   How an egg gets created.

| KEY POINT | There isn't "real" and "unreal" in your hologram. |

Everything in your hologram is unreal. *Everything* is just a belief.

This is also the explanation of why positive thinking, affirmations, and other popular self-help strategies and techniques don't work consistently. You can think positive thoughts, visualize, or affirm all day long, but if your Expanded Self doesn't create a pattern in The Field that matches what you *appear* to be thinking, visualizing, or affirming, and add enormous power to it, it can't pop into your hologram. It doesn't matter how many times you think it, how many times you visualize the outcome manifesting, how many times you repeat an affirmation to yourself or hear it on tape, or how much you as the Persona believe it to be true. It's going to fall flat without a corresponding change to a pattern in The Field. Conversely, if you remove all your power from a pattern, the pattern collapses, and whatever that pattern was creating in your hologram disappears from your hologram.

| KEY POINT | There's no power in the hologram. All the power comes from you and is stored in a pattern in The Field, the true source of everything in your hologram—including you as the Persona or star of your total immersion movie. |

Have you ever seen a video of a building being demolished—where the entire structure collapses in a matter of seconds or minutes? The initial creation of a building must be done piece by piece, brick by brick, beam by beam, and it takes months or years. But collapsing it is accomplished in seconds or minutes. Why? Because they put explosive charges in strategic places within the building to undermine the core foundation of the building. When those charges are detonated, the building collapses rapidly. If you've never seen a video like that, visit the following page on my web site to see an example. It's a very powerful visual image to have in your mind as you bust loose from The Money Game:

http://www.bustingloose.com/dynamite.html

It works the same way in Phase 2 of The Human Game. Your Expanded Self knows where the eggs with the most power in them are "hidden" in The Field, what's in them, which ones are limiting you the most, and so on. In Phase 2, your Expanded Self guides you to those "foundational eggs" and supports you in reclaiming the power from them, dissolving the judgment and consequences, collapsing the patterns, and therefore removing the limitation they contained from your hologram. Just like with demolishing a building, you don't need to collapse all the patterns you created in Phase 1—just the key foundational ones. To bust loose from The Money Game, you'll do exactly that with the eggs you created to limit the natural flow of abundance to you. That's why I call it The Treasure Hunt of the Century. What more valuable treasure could you ever find than opening up fully into the Infinite Abundance and raw creative power that's your natural state?

| KEY POINT | It takes much *less* time to reclaim power in Phase 2 than it took to hide it in Phase 1.

When treasure hunters hunt for treasure, either above ground or under water, they use specific tools. You too must use specific tools to participate in The Treasure Hunt of the Century and bust loose from The Money Game. To discover what they are and how to use them, turn the page and begin Chapter 9.

Jumping into the Driver's Seat

*Inspiration is everywhere. If you're ready to appreciate it, an
ant can be one of the wonders of the universe.*[1]

—Author Unknown

*It is far more delightful to be fond of the world because it
has thousands of aspects and is different everywhere . . . for
every divergence deserves to be cherished, simply because it
widens the bounds of life.*[2]

—Karel Capek, Writer (1890–1938)

C ars have driver's seats and passenger's seats. Passengers have
no power or control over what happens in the car. Drivers
have all the power and control. In Phase 1 of The Human
Game, you (the Persona) were in the passenger's seat. In Phase 2,

you have the opportunity to jump into the driver's seat. When you want to drive a car to a specific destination, the first thing you do is get into the driver's seat and buckle your seat belt. That's what we're going to do now as you prepare to launch yourself into Phase 2 of The Human Game.

There are four tools you'll use to play in Phase 2 of The Human Game and bust loose from The Money Game. I'm going to introduce all four tools in this chapter, discuss the first tool in detail, then we'll discuss the other three tools in Chapter 10. Here are your four treasure-hunting tools:

1. Expressing Appreciation
2. The Process
3. The Mini-Process
4. Empowering Vocabulary and Self-Talk

All four tools are extremely powerful and necessary parts of the Busting Loose Process. However, of the four, The Process, which we'll discuss in the next chapter, is the crown jewel—the one you'll use the most, and the one with the most transformative power at the start of your journey. However, before you can apply The Process, you must first discover the magic of Expressing Appreciation, so that's where we'll begin our discussion.

Expressing Appreciation

If you're like most people, you were taught that the purpose of money is to provide an efficient means of exchange for goods and services. You were taught civilizations once bartered for goods and services, but that became awkward and inefficient so money was created to make the process simpler and easier. You were also taught that the process of exchanging money became easier and more efficient as we moved from coins to bills to credit cards to electronic funds transfer. However, like everything else in Phase 1 of The Human Game, what you were taught was just a smokescreen, a cloud, an illusion designed to trick you and lock you into limitation and restriction.

When somebody does something nice or helpful for you, or you receive something of value from another person, how do you respond? You say "Thank you," right? You express appreciation for the value you received. If you go into a store, restaurant, or other place of business and *pay* for something, aren't you also receiving something of value? Don't you also say thank you in such circumstances—if you're a well-mannered person?

If money disappeared from the planet tomorrow, what would change? Would books disappear from the shelves in bookstores? Would restaurants and shops close? Would cars stop rolling off the assembly lines? Would doctor's offices, gas stations, dry cleaners, and copy shops close their doors? Would *any* good or service that you now enjoy or benefit from suddenly become unavailable?

No!

So, if money disappeared but you could still obtain goods and services, what would still be there in the *transaction?*

The expression of appreciation.

You'd still want to say thank you to the people who provided the good or service for you. You'd receive something valuable and you'd want to express appreciation for it. If you went into a restaurant and had a great time, you'd say thank you to the server who waited on you. If you went into a dress shop and *bought* a beautiful gown, you'd say thank you to the clerk or owner. If you went into an electronics store and *bought* a computer or cell phone, you'd say thank you after receiving it.

Every *bill* you *pay* is for something valuable you received. You may not like *paying* your rent or mortgage, but having a place to live is valuable isn't it? You may not like *paying back* a loan, but the money you were loaned allowed you to buy or do something valuable. You may not like the total you see, but if your credit card *bill* has 10 items on it, when you received or experienced each of those

10 things, you received value, didn't you? If you look closely with your Phase 2 X-ray vision, whenever you *pay* for anything, all you're *really* doing is saying, "Thank you, I appreciate what I've received."

| KEY POINT | Whenever you create and experience the illusion of receiving a |

good, service, or experience in your hologram, there are three aspects of the creation to appreciate:

1. Yourself for how amazing you had to be to make the illusion appear so real.
2. Your creation—be it person, place, or thing—for how amazingly real it seems, how perfectly he, she, or it is supporting you in playing The Human Game, and the specific benefit you received from it (the enjoyment of the meal, clothing, race, mountain climb, glass of champagne, and so on).
3. The Creative Process that made 1 and 2 possible.

Based on what you now know about The Human Game, if you eat dinner in a restaurant and *pay* with cash, check, or credit card, who are you paying? Yourself, right? There's no one else "out there" to pay. Everything and everyone is a creation of *your Consciousness.* So, who is ultimately providing the value and who are you really saying thank you to?

Yourself!

As you know, in the restaurant example I've been using, there's no restaurant. Your Consciousness is creating the illusion of it—the room, tables, chairs, art on the walls, music playing in the background, kitchen, food, plates, glasses, waiter, busperson, chef, the other people who appear to be eating there with you (extras, if we use the movie analogy), everyone and everything else you experience while you're there. None of it is really there, yet, you convince yourself it's all there and all real. That's an incredible accomplishment, so take the opportunity to fully appreciate it!

| KEY POINT | The real purpose of money is to express appreciation for the |

The real purpose of money is to express appreciation for the magnificence of yourself as the Creator of everything you experience and the magnificence of all your creations as you create and experience them.

If you're like many of the people I work with, a thought like the following may have just popped into your mind (or will later): "I can't go around patting myself on the back like that or calling myself magnificent. That would be egotistical and self-centered." Whether you just had a thought like that or not, follow along with me here for a moment because it's likely it will come up later. Do you remember what I said the purpose of Phase 1 in The Human Game is? To convince yourself you're the exact opposite of who you really are. This is a perfect example of that. Look at how brilliant and tricky we are as Creators. Who you are is a magnificent and Infinite Being, yet in Phase 1, you succeeded in convincing yourself that to feel that way and see that Truth is egotistical or self-centered, either of which is a synonym for a judgment called "bad." Every time I turn on my X-ray vision to see The Human Game clearly, I come away in absolute awe of what an amazing Game it is and how amazing we have to be as players to make it work.

Do you ever run out of love? If you love your child or significant other and you express that love verbally, through a kiss, a touch, or a gift of some kind, do you have less love afterward? Does the amount of love you have or your capacity to express it diminish?

No!

In fact, if you look closely, you have an endless supply of love, and every time you express it, your capacity to express—and receive—love actually expands. It works the same way with appreciation and expressing appreciation in the form of money. You have an endless supply of appreciation and every time you express it, your capacity to express—and receive—appreciation expands, too. Therefore, as you dramatically increase your expression of appreciation, what must happen as a result? The flow of appreciation that comes back to you *in the form of money* must expand, too—and that's exactly what happens when you play in Phase 2 of The Human Game!

KEY POINT	**Your supply of money does *not* decrease as you spend. It actually loops back and then increases.**

Now that you understand the concept of appreciation and the power it holds, let's take a look at its practical application. Then we'll further enhance it when I show you how appreciation ties into the crown jewel tool called *The Process* in the next chapter. What's it like now for you when you pay bills? When I ask that question at my live events, here's what I hear most often:

> "It's scary because I don't always have enough in my checking account, and if I don't pay or my check bounces, I'm in trouble."

> "When I pay a bill for one thing it means I won't have money to do something else I'd like to do. It's an either/or deal and I don't like that."

> "I just feel resigned to the fact that what I have is going to be depleted by the amount I have to pay."

> "For me, it's a gigantic hassle. I could be doing something else. I don't like spending time writing out checks, putting them in envelopes, putting stamps on them, and putting them in the mail."

> "I feel powerless when I pay bills, and I don't like feeling that way so I compensate by putting off paying, which leads to late fees, which leads to anger at myself for being so stupid."

> "I don't mind paying bills, but paying taxes drives me nuts. It just doesn't seem right. It seems unjust. It's my money. I made it. Why does the government get to take so much of it whether I like it or not?"

Whether you have similar thoughts and feelings or other *nega-tive* thoughts and feelings when you *pay bills*, what's being reinforced when you think and feel that way? Three things:

1. Your beliefs about the limits on your power and abundance
2. Your judgment of those beliefs
3. The reality of the consequences you have associated with them

In effect, you're making your financial limitation eggs larger and larger, and when you do that, the financial limitation must persist in your hologram. If you'd describe your feelings as neutral or flat when you *pay bills*, you may not be reinforcing limitation, but you're missing an opportunity to reclaim power and shrink the egg as you'll soon see.

The opportunity you give yourself in Phase 2 of The Human Game is to shift your focus from *paying bills* to expressing appreciation. Doing that will take self-discipline and persistence in the beginning, because it will feel alien to you, but it ultimately becomes natural and "old hat" to you. Starting now, every time you *pay bills*, write checks, hand someone cash, or sign a credit card slip, you want to take a moment to appreciate your creation, yourself as the Creator of it, and the value you received.

How to Express Appreciation instead of Pay Bills

Ninety percent of the time I express appreciation with a credit card. So when I sign credit card slips or write checks when I receive credit card *bills* in the mail (which I now call "requests for appreciation," which is a preview of the Empowering Vocabulary and Self-Talk tool), I look at the *bill* or go down every line item on the statement and express appreciation for the creations they represent.

For example, suppose I'm looking at a credit card slip for dinner at one of my favorite sushi restaurants after finishing a fine meal. I then express appreciation by saying words like this to myself *and feeling the genuine feelings that accompany them:* "Wow! What an amazing creation. I created this whole thing—the restaurant, the waiter, the sushi, the sushi chef, the sake I drank, the table I sat at, and the other people in the restaurant. It was all a creation of my Consciousness. It all seemed so real and tasted so good! Amazing. I'm one hell of a Creator!" As I sign the slip, I then conclude by saying something like this to myself: "I express this appreciation from the Infinite Abundance that's my natural state, knowing that as I make that expression the abundance I experience in my hologram expands and returns to me."

If you've had experience using the self-help technique called affirmations, a thought like this may have just crossed your mind: "That sounds just like using affirmations. I thought you said affirmations have no power." In Phase 1, without a corresponding pattern in The Field that gets energized, affirmations have no power. Plus, most people affirm for things they don't really believe are true or possible for them. However, when you affirm The Truth in Phase 2, it *does* have power because your Expanded Self is helping you expand and reclaim your power so new patterns *do get created* in The Field to support the effort. I'll discuss this in greater detail in the next chapter.

I'd do the same thing if I created what could be judged a bad experience in the restaurant from a Phase 1 perspective. Why? Because, as we discussed, there's no power in the hologram—not in anything, not in anyone. The other people are actors saying and doing what I asked them to say and do. The food is entirely a creation of my Consciousness, so if I experienced what could be called poor service or lousy food, I created that illusion from a pattern in The Field and convinced myself it was real—which is a colossal achievement—and definitely something to appreciate.

KEY POINT The words you say to yourself to express appreciation don't matter. It's the feelings the words help you create within yourself that count.

I gave you examples of the words I use when expressing appreciation. I change them all the time. There isn't any rule or magic formula for expressing appreciation. There's no right way, wrong way, better way, or best way. None of that exists in Phase 2. There's just what you choose to do, and what generates truly appreciative feelings. You can always trust yourself and your Expanded Self and just say and do what you feel motivated to say and do.

What happens when you express appreciation like this instead of *paying bills* like you do now? Two things:

1. It starts the process of draining power from the financially limiting eggs you installed in The Field in Phase 1 (which we'll be discussing in the next chapter).

2. It sets into motion the circular flow of increased appreciation to you that means more appreciation flowing to you in the form of money.

Here's another way to look at this. Suppose you went to Las Vegas and played the slot machines. Suppose you found a slot machine that immediately returned three dollars for every dollar you put into it. How many dollars would you put into that machine? As many as you could, right? How would you feel every time you put a dollar in the machine? Excited, right? Because you knew three dollars would be coming back. It's the same thing when you express appreciation instead of *pay bills*, and you really get into the energy of appreciating yourself, your creations, and the value you receive from your creations. You now know that each time you *pay a bill* you actually end up getting more money back than the amount you expressed. As a result, once you bust loose from The Money Game, you actually enjoy and look forward to *paying bills* instead of dreading it or having the *negative* sort of experience you have now.

When you express appreciation, you must really feel it. You can't fake it. You can't bluff your way through it because who are you trying to bluff? Yourself! You can't be sitting there and say, "This sucks, but Bob said I should appreciate it, so okay, I appreciate you soooo much. There, it's done. Onward and upward." Really feeling it is what takes time, practice, and discipline. However, the value created from it is absolutely off the charts and well worth any amount of time and effort that are required.

Do you resonate with this and really get it? Or does it sound crazy to you, like pie in the sky or like I must be on some sort of drug? Regardless of your thoughts at the moment, I assure you, if you really feel it and really do it, you'll see the expansion of abundance effect for yourself. I've seen it. I continue to see it, and I've seen it in my clients, some of whose stories I'll be sharing in Chapter 12.

Here's another example. Let's say tomorrow morning you stop at a coffee shop on the way to work and *buy* yourself a vanilla latte for $4.00. As you give the clerk the $4.00, you could say something like this to yourself—and really *feel* it—"Wow, this is so cool. I created this coffee shop. I created the espresso machine, the beans, the milk, the steamer, the syrup, and the cup. I created the clerk and all the people who appeared to be in the coffee shop with me." Then, as you sip the sweet, hot liquid, you could say—and feel—"Wow!" again. Why? Because there's no coffee shop, no espresso machine, no beans, no milk, no steamer, no syrup, no cup, and no hot, sweet liquid. It's all smoke and mirrors. All an illusion. You just convinced yourself it was there, it was real, and it tasted good.

THAT'S AN AMAZING, MAGNIFICENT, MAGICAL, MIND-BLOWING, "SUPERNATURAL" ACCOMPLISHMENT! APPRECIATE IT!

In Phase 2 of The Human Game, besides shifting your focus from *paying bills* to expressing appreciation, there are two additional opportunities you can give yourself that support you in busting loose from The Money Game. First, you can give yourself the gift of appreciating all the money you appear to receive from others. Right now, when you receive a paycheck, a royalty check, a dividend check, or other expression of appreciation in the form of money, how do you respond? Do you feel tremendous appreciation for it— for yourself as the Creator, the creation, and the creative process?

Or, do you take it for granted, swear under your breath because the check wasn't larger, or instantly compare the amount to your *bills* or your wants and find it lacking? No matter what your current response is, you now have the opportunity to convert it to an expression of appreciation and start getting the three dollars back for every one dollar you put in the slot machine, to continue that metaphor.

For example, I own and run several businesses and have partnerships in several others. In Phase 1 of The Human Game, I looked at those businesses and the *payments* I received from them as the source of my financial abundance. In Phase 2, I know they're *not* the source of my abundance (my Consciousness is), but I still express appreciation to myself in the form of money from them. Here's how I do it. When I write myself a check from one of the company accounts or receive a check from one of my partnerships, I follow the same steps I just outlined. Why? Because the checks aren't real, the companies aren't real, the customers who *bought* products and services that gave the companies the money to be able to *pay* me aren't real, it's all just a magnificent creation and illusion, and I appreciate it.

Beyond my businesses and partnerships, I also receive royalties on books I've written and audio albums I've recorded that are published and sold by others, plus other commissions and other financial rewards of various kinds. When I receive those checks, I express appreciation for them, too.

The second additional opportunity you can give yourself is to fully appreciate what you've already created and are enjoying in your hologram versus judging it, taking it for granted, or focusing on what you don't have. If you judge what you currently have by saying it's bad, not enough, it sucks, it's not what you want, you want more, you want something different, or the like, what are you doing? Reinforcing the illusion that it's real and that you really are limited. If you focus on what you don't have what are you doing? Same thing.

Everything you're currently experiencing in your hologram is there because your Expanded Self created a complex pattern in The

Field, energized it, and popped it into your hologram making it appear absolutely real. There was no accident or mistake. Whatever you've experienced and are experiencing now was brilliantly designed and popped into your hologram to perfectly support you in playing The Human Game exactly the way you wanted to play it— *no matter how you'd judge or label it from your old perspective*. It deserves to be appreciated for all its magnificence! You can create anything you choose once you move deeply enough into Phase 2, but first you must appreciate what you've already created. If you don't appreciate what you've already created, why would your Expanded Self support you by creating more "stuff" you won't appreciate either? If you don't appreciate what you've already created, it's like putting a dollar into the slot machine and getting nothing back. Why do that when you can get three dollars back instead?

> **KEY POINT**   It's possible and very easy to fully appreciate what you already have, even if you may choose to create something else at another time.

By the way, just as a sidebar before we conclude this chapter, do you think it's any accident that the term *appreciation* is used in the traditional financial community to describe an increase in value in an investment or portfolio? As part of Phase 1 in The Human Game, we hide clues to The Truth all over the place but make sure we don't "see" them. If you make the leap into Phase 2, you'll see clues like that everywhere and find it quite amusing and fascinating.

When you're ready to receive The Process—the crown jewel that you'll combine with appreciation to reclaim your power from the patterns/eggs you've installed in The Field to limit the flow of financial abundance to yourself, turn the page to begin Chapter 10.

CHAPTER

10

Putting Your Foot on the Gas

Sometimes a person has to go back, really back—to have a sense, an understanding, of all that's gone to make them— before they can go forward.[1]

—Paule Marshall, Poet and Writer

Life is one-tenth Here and Now, nine-tenths a history lesson. For most of the time, the Here and Now is neither now nor here.[2]

—Graham Swift, *Waterland*, Vintage

In the previous chapter, by moving into the practical side of the Busting Loose Process and discovering the magic of Appreciation, you jumped into the driver's seat and buckled your seatbelt in preparation for a fast and wild ride into Phase 2 of The Human

95

Game. To expand on that metaphor, it's time to put the key in the ignition, start the car, put your foot on the gas, and start accelerating toward busting loose from The Money Game.

In this chapter, you'll be discovering the second, third, and fourth treasure hunting tools, including *The Process* that was designed to support you in reclaiming power from the eggs in The Field that have been limiting you (including financially). It's the crown jewel of the Busting Loose Process. The Process is the accelerator that rockets you out of Phase 1, into Phase 2, and out of The Money Game, completely and permanently. It's the most extraordinary tool I've ever developed or experienced. Being able to apply The Process is what all the preceding chapters and puzzle pieces have been building to and what you ultimately came to this book to receive. However, as you'll see, an explanation of The Process would not have made any sense and you wouldn't have been able to apply it without the foundation of the other puzzle pieces that were delivered in previous chapters.

Applying The Process to reclaim power is easy. It's also a lot of fun once you get your feet wet and become comfortable with it. Like learning any other new skill, however, it may feel strange and awkward at first. Let me make one point clear before we continue. As the Infinite Being that you really are, you have the power to snap your fingers and instantly have all your power, wisdom, and abundance back. However, that's not how Phase 2 of The Human Game was designed to be played. It was designed to be played so you'd reclaim your power, wisdom, and abundance one piece at a time so you could savor each returning piece—and the expansion it creates for you—like you'd savor a fine wine, a fine meal, a great play, or novel.

Because of your limiting experiences in Phase 1 of The Human Game and your frustration with them, it's understandable that you'd want all your power, wisdom, and abundance back instantaneously, especially when you get a taste of what's possible in Phase 2. I felt that way too when I first entered Phase 2. However, you must understand that it doesn't work that way—nor would you want it to. If you entered Phase 2 and instantly reclaimed all your power, wisdom, and abundance, it would be the equivalent of scheduling the Super Bowl between the Denver Broncos and the Seattle Seahawks, getting all the players, coaches, referees, support staff, and fans at the stadium and having millions watching on television worldwide, then having the referee snap his fingers and say "Okay, the Denver Broncos just won 37 to 10. You can all go home now."

The players don't want to go home. The coaches, referees, and support staff don't want to go home. The fans don't want to go home. Everyone wants all four quarters of the game to be played, no matter what ups and downs might be experienced, how difficult the playing might get, or what the final outcome is. The players want to play because they love the game. Well, as a player in The Human Game, you don't want to go home the minute you enter Phase 2 either (even though part of you might say you do). You want to play because the Real You loves The Human Game.

The Process is used to reclaim your power from the limiting eggs you created and installed in The Field in Phase 1. Power is hidden inside *all* your creations, inside everything you see and experience in your hologram, inside every aspect of what you call your daily life. However, the greatest amount of power is hidden where you feel discomfort. As you now know, who you really are is an Infinite Being who's in a constant state of joyfulness, peace, and unconditional love for everything and everyone. As such, it's impossible for the Real You to have discomfort of any kind. It's *impossible* for the Real You to feel fear, anxiety, embarrassment, shame, anger, or anything else you'd label as a *negative* emotion.

The only way you can appear to feel discomfort is if you create a pattern in The Field, add an enormous amount of power to it, pop the illusion of it into your hologram, and convince yourself it's real. And the more discomfort you feel, the more *negative* you feel, the more intense the *negative* emotions are, the further away from who you really are you pushed yourself, the harder you had to work to convince yourself the illusion was real, and the more power you had to use to pull it off. Therefore, to support you in reclaiming the greatest amount of power from the most strategically placed eggs in The Field, your Expanded Self will activate patterns that pop extremely uncomfortable situations into your hologram for you to experience and apply The Process to.

As we discussed in Chapter 2, from the moment you were born, you began hiding your tremendous power, wisdom, and abundance from yourself and convincing yourself you were the complete opposite of who you really are. You also convinced yourself most of the hiding places were so painful, dangerous, scary, and deadly that they had to be avoided at all costs. You convinced yourself if you "went there" something horrible would happen—you'd die, lose yourself, lose your marriage or kids, be shamed or embarrassed beyond your ability to cope, whatever it is. You know what "don't go there" emotions feel like because you've experienced them throughout your life. In Phase 2, your Expanded Self will take you back to those places, keep you absolutely safe, and support you in reclaiming your power from them.

Once you've applied The Process enough and reclaimed enough power, your hologram changes, then it changes some more, then the pace of change starts to accelerate, which is when it gets really exciting. As you reclaim more and more power and collapse more and more limiting patterns in The Field, the power, wisdom, and abundance that's your natural state starts shining through more and more, and your life becomes more and more "miraculous."

Here's how it works. Your Expanded Self guides you to the scary eggs and pops them open so you can feel the power in them—the power you had to put there to keep the illusion of limitation in place. While the eggs are open and the power is available, your Expanded Self then guides you to apply The Process to reclaim as much power as is desirable at that moment. Remember, the goal is not to get all your power back instantly, but over time. Each time you reclaim power, you expand and more becomes possible for you. Each time you reclaim power, you change as a person. One expansion leads to the next that leads to the next in a chain reaction that ultimately dynamites and collapses the "limitation machine" you built in Phase 1. That's when you bust loose from The Money Game.

I'm now going to explain how to apply The Process. Please keep in mind a very important point: There's a core structure to The Process, and there are guidelines for how to work within that structure. The core structure must be respected each time you apply The Process. If you don't respect the core structure, it won't support you in reclaiming power. However, the guidelines for working within the structure are just that—guidelines—and you have a lot of freedom and wiggle room to modify them to your liking. In short, there's no one way, best way, rule, or magic formula for how to apply The Process. Like everything in The Human Game, it must be customized for your unique needs as a unique Infinite Being on a unique mission.

I'll highlight the core structural components for you and share the guidelines I've developed for myself, my clients, and students, then I encourage you to follow the lead of your Expanded Self as you evolve The Process for yourself, play with it, experiment, and make it your own. That's what I did. What I do now and what I did when I first started applying The Process are very different. I'm now going to give you an overview of the steps for applying The Process, then we'll discuss each step in detail. Remember, it will all start with experiences being popped into your hologram that cause you discomfort—perhaps great, perhaps minor.

An Overview of The Process

When you experience discomfort of any kind:

- Dive right smack into the middle of it.
- Feel the discomfort energy fully.
- When it reaches a peak of intensity, tell The Truth about it.
- Reclaim your power from it.

- Open up more and more to who you *really* are.
- Express appreciation for yourself and the creation.

The key here is to apply The Process *each time* you feel discomfort, especially as it relates to money and finances. That means if you feel discomfort *because* the stock market drops and with it the value of your portfolio. Or you feel discomfort when you get an unexpected *bill*. Or you look at a *price tag* for an item in a store or the *prices* on a wine list in a restaurant, or a per-night *rate* for a hotel stay, or whatever it is and you wince or say "That's too expensive." Or you feel discomfort as you have experiences and ask yourself questions like these:

- "Can I afford that?"
- "Should I buy that?"
- "Would it be prudent to buy that right now?"
- "Do I really need that right now?"
- "What would my spouse think if I bought or did that?"

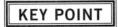 If you feel any form of discomfort at all, you apply The Process.

Step 1: Dive Right Smack into the Middle of It

The tremendous power that's disguised as discomfort is very real and very tangible. You can feel it. You might experience it as a gigantic vibrating ball of energy. You might experience it as feeling like a hurricane or tornado of energy. It might feel like a whirlpool or vortex of rushing water. It doesn't matter how you experience it. We're all different and have different ways of experiencing emotions, energy, and power. Just notice what's there for you. Whatever your experience of the discomfort is, *in Consciousness*, you dive right into the middle of it (or run or walk or jump or whatever action works for you). However you choose to do it, fully immerse yourself within the discomfort energy. In the beginning, it will be easier if you apply The Process with your eyes closed. Later, it won't matter and you'll be able to do it on the fly, even while engaged in conversation with others.

Step 2: Feel the Discomfort Energy Fully

Once you're fully immersed in the discomfort energy, feel it as fully as you possibly can. Just feel it, the intensity, the waves, the raw power in it, whatever it feels like for you. If you can escalate the intensity and allow yourself to feel even more of what's there, do it because the more you feel, the more power you can reclaim. I say this because in Phase 1, many of us create a dynamic where we automatically decrease the intensity of all our emotions before we allow ourselves to feel them. For example, the true intensity of the emotion might be at level 100, but we knock it down to level 60 before we allow ourselves to feel it because that feels safer. Therefore, in that example, there would actually be 40 additional units of power available we're not generally consciously aware of. You have the opportunity to reclaim power from all the available units when you apply The Process. If you feel comfortable doing it, do it. If you don't, no big deal. You can go back and get the rest of the power later.

> **KEY POINT** Just feel the energy of the discomfort as much as you'll allow yourself to. No thinking, no logic, no intellect, no judgment, no labeling. Just *feel* it.

The intensity you feel, no matter how you might judge or label it, is your power. It's who you really are. It's what you had to put in the egg/pattern to pop that experience into your hologram and convince yourself it was real. If you get to the point where you feel like you're going to be overwhelmed by the energy, you can stop, but I invite you to stretch yourself. The feelings of danger are just an old trick you used in Phase 1 to keep yourself away from your power. You can ignore the trick—completely safely—if you choose to. Your Expanded Self is always protecting you and keeping you safe and would never give you more than you can handle, no matter how it appears.

The core structural component of step two is feeling the feelings as fully as you possibly can. *How* you do it, what you see, feel, hear, and create for yourself in the experience is all up to you and you can evolve and change what you do over time. As I've explained, there are no rules or formulas for anything in Phase 2 of The Human Game.

Step 3: When It Reaches a Peak of Intensity, Tell The Truth about It

As you immerse yourself in the discomfort energy and feel it as fully as you possibly can, you'll notice the energy reaching its own natural peak of intensity—or you'll notice yourself reaching the limit of how much you're willing to feel in that moment. Trust yourself on knowing when the peak or your limit has been reached. Resist the Phase 1 temptation to get overly analytical and beat yourself up by saying something like this to yourself, "I have to find the perfect peak point, and if I miss it I screwed it up and I'm an idiot." You just do your best and trust your Expanded Self, especially at the start. It'll get easier as you apply The Process more and more.

When the intensity reaches its peak, you call it what it really is, which means you tell The Truth about it. What does that mean? You affirm who you really are, how powerful you really are, that you created it, it's not real, just a creation of your Consciousness. To do that, you must come up with a phrase to describe the Real You that resonates with you and supports you in feeling as powerful and infinite as you possibly can. Following are some examples you can use or adapt, or you can make up your own phrase. The words don't matter. How they make you *feel* is the only thing that matters. The first phrase is what I use. It's a phrase that was given to me by Arnold Patent and I liked it so I use it. The others are examples of phrases my clients and students use:

"I am the Power and Presence of God."
"I am the Power of Infinite Intelligence."
"I am the Power of Pure Consciousness."
"I am the Ultimate Power in the Universe."

Once you choose a phrase, and it may change and evolve over time, you then add your affirmation of The Truth after it and expand the phrase. For example, this is what I say in step three of The Process:

"I am the Power and Presence of God creating this. It's not real. It's completely made up. It's a creation of *my* Consciousness."

The core structural component of step 3 is telling The Truth about your creation and whatever appears to be causing it. You must tell The Truth about it and really *feel* the truthfulness and power of the words you use to describe it. Why? Because throughout Phase 1, you lied to yourself about it. You told yourself the illusion was real, it was scary, it had power and you did not, and those lies locked you into limitation. When you apply The Process, you must reverse that trend and call it what it really is. How you do it, what words you use, and how you use them is up to you.

Step 4: Reclaim Your Power from It

After you tell The Truth about your creation, you then simply reclaim your power from it by affirming it using words like this: "I reclaim my power from this creation NOW!" Those are the words I used at the beginning of my Phase 2 journey. However, I later added the following wording to that first sentence: "As I reclaim that power, I feel it coming back to me." (And I really feel it "flowing" back to me.) Then I say, "I feel it surging through me." (And I feel it surging through me.)

Reclaiming the power in step 4 is a critical step in The Process, especially at the start. Steps 5 and 6 are also important, and will become more and more important as you move more deeply into Phase 2, but as you'll see, they may take some time to master. If you follow steps 1 through 4, you *will* reclaim power and your hologram *will* change.

Step 5: Open Up More and More to Who You *Really* Are

In step 5, you open up to The Truth and Power of who you really are, and you really feel it. I call this *feeling the Infinite Energy*. For purposes of discussion, suppose you chose to use the same description I do for who you really are: "The Power and Presence of God." You must then learn to cultivate the feeling of really *being* that—the feeling of actually *being* infinitely powerful, infinitely wise, and infinitely abundant. You start by asking yourself questions like these, "What would it feel like if I had infinite power, wisdom, and abundance? What would it feel like if I could just snap my fingers and anything I wanted instantly manifested? What would it feel like to be in absolute joyfulness and peace all the time?"

The way I was able to cultivate and expand those feelings was by repeating the following phrases to myself, over and over, and feeling, really feeling, the Truth and power of them:

I am the Power and Presence of God creating everything I experience, everything.

There's no power out there, not in anyone, not in anything.

I am in Infinite Abundance, right here, right now.

Infinite power to create anything I want.

Infinite knowledge and wisdom.

Infinite feelings of joyfulness and peace.

Infinite feelings of unconditional love and appreciation for all my creations.

Infinite supply of money to express appreciation with, right here, right now.

There's no magic to it, but as I say those words, I also raise my hands and arms, palms up, so when I'm at the end and saying "right here, right now," my open palms are above my head. For me, the feeling of rising movement as I feel the power expand within me is supportive.

Now, in your present state, you don't know what it actually feels like to be an Infinite Being who possesses all the qualities I just listed. You don't remember what the Infinite Energy feels like. So, you do your best at the start with full confidence that your capacity to feel the Infinite Energy will expand over time. If you use words like I did, they may seem empty and hollow at first. That's okay. Say them anyway. If you use another strategy to feel the Infinite Energy, it may feel weak at first. That's okay, too. Just do your best and resist the Phase 1 temptation to beat yourself up for not doing it perfectly, for getting "better" too slowly, doubting yourself or The Process. Your goal is to be able to feel the Infinite Energy on command—and you *will* get there if you commit to playing in Phase 2 of The Human Game. And remember, you're not alone when you do the Phase 2 work. Your Expanded Self is always there with you, helping you and supporting you perfectly at all times.

| KEY POINT | In the beginning, everything may sound like empty words. That's okay. Say them anyway and feel them as much as you can. Over time, they become more and more and more real to you—naturally. |

Coming back to The Process, after you affirm that you've reclaimed the power from your creation in step 4, you then open up into the Infinite Energy and immerse yourself in it. Here's what I say—and feel—as I do it:

> "As I feel the surge, I feel myself expanding more and more into who I really am. I feel myself expressing more and more of who I really am in my hologram, in my Human Experience . . . I AM the Power and Presence of God. I AM in Infinite Abundance, right here right now."

KEY POINT	You must always really *feel* The Truth behind the words you use!

Then, while immersed in the Infinite Energy, *in Consciousness,* you replay the experience that triggered the original discomfort. If you still feel any discomfort as you experience the scene again, merge the discomfort energy into the Infinite Energy and let the discomfort dissolve into the Infinite Energy. Replay the scene as many times as you feel moved to and merge it into the Infinite Energy until you can replay it, and feel only the Infinite Energy.

Step 6: Express Appreciation

In the sixth and final step, you take a look at the "movie scene" you created to stimulate the feelings of discomfort, and you appreciate how magnificent that creation was, how amazing you had to be to create it, and how amazing it is that you could actually believe it was real when it was really just smoke and mirrors. In essence, you want to say and feel "WOW!" about the creation you just reclaimed power from and bask in the why of that wow and in all your magnificence. I call this "The Wow Effect." Therefore, at the end of applying The Process, you're in an extremely joyous and expanded state.

Making It Work

Does this seem too simple? If so, the reason is it's not just about what you're doing. You're applying The Process side-by-side with your Expanded Self who is leading you to the eggs, popping them open for you, and helping you take the power back from them. That's how The Human Game works. In Phase 1, your Expanded Self did everything in His/Her power to keep you away from your power. In Phase 2, He/She does everything in His/Her power to help you reclaim it and expand. By applying The Process, over time, you drain the power from the eggs that have been limiting the flow of financial abundance to you. You also dissolve the beliefs, judgments, and consequences stored in them.

Does The Process seem confusing or overwhelming to you? If so, it won't after you start using it for a while with the help of your Expanded Self. I've taught The Process to thousands of people all over the world. It always takes some practice, but everyone "gets it" quickly and then evolves it over time to make it their own. You will too! The toughest parts, from my experience (and they may be easy for you since we're all different) are finding the courage to dive into the discomfort the first few times when it still appears scary, fully appreciating a creation you previously judged, and learning to cultivate the Infinite Energy to open up to at the end. However, all of it will come in time with just a little practice.

Here are the guidelines for applying The Process again for easy reference and review. When you hit the peak of intensity with any discomfort you feel, you dive into the heart of the discomfort and say:

"I am _____ creating this." (Fill in the blank with the description you chose.)

"It's not real." (Really feel the meaning of the words.)

"It's completely made up." (Really feel the meaning of the words.)

"It's a creation of my Consciousness." (Really feel the meaning of the words.)

"I reclaim my power from this creation NOW."

"As I reclaim the power, I feel it coming back to me." (Feel it.)

"I feel it surging through me." (Really feel it surging.)

"As I feel the surge, I feel myself expanding more and more into who I really am, expressing more and more of who I really am in my Human Experience. I am _____." (Insert the description you chose.)

Fully appreciate how amazing you had to be to create this and convince yourself it was real, how amazing the creation was, and how beautifully it served you in Phase 1.

Let's now go through The Process with a specific example. Feel free to create your own example as we go along if the one I share doesn't work for you in terms of bringing up discomfort. Suppose you take your car to the shop for routine maintenance, and the service rep tells you there's a serious problem you must resolve immediately. She also tells you it will *cost* $2,500 to repair. Further suppose that in the illusion, you've convinced yourself you don't have enough money in your checking account to *pay* for the repair. As the service rep tells you the "good news," you tighten up and feel fear or another form of intense discomfort.

At the moment you feel the discomfort in the situation, *in Consciousness*, you dive right into the middle of the discomfort and feel it as fully as you can. Allow it to reach its natural peak or your personal feeling limit in the moment. When you feel the peak, you say your equivalent of my words and *really feel them:*

"I am the Power and Presence of God creating this. It's not real. It's completely made up. It's a creation of *my* Consciousness, and I reclaim my power from this creation NOW." Then you pause briefly and continue, "As I reclaim the power, I feel it coming back to me." And you pause to feel it coming back to you, however that feels to you. "I feel it surging through me." Then you pause to feel the surge. "As I feel it surging through me, I feel myself expanding even more into who I really am, expressing even more of who I really am—_____," as you feel yourself opening up into The Infinite Energy.

Then, in Consciousness, you replay the scene where the service rep told you about the $2,500 repair. If you feel any discomfort as you replay it (and you may or may not), take that discomfort and dissolve it into the Infinite Energy and repeat that step until there's no more discomfort. Then bask in the Infinite Energy for as long as you feel so moved. Then appreciate how amazing it was that you created the illusion of a car, a problem with the car, a repair shop and the service rep, the illusion of you not having the money to *pay* for it when your abundance is infinite, and that you convinced yourself it was all real when none of it was. You appreciate yourself as the Creator, you appreciate the creation, and you appreciate the value you received from it (which in this example would be the Phase 2 opportunity to reclaim power and reaffirm The Truth).

That's it. That's The Process. After you get comfortable with it, depending on the details in the "movie scene" that triggered the discomfort and the personal choices you make in applying The Process, the whole thing can take as little as a minute or as long as you choose to extend it. It ultimately becomes quick and easy. It doesn't take hours or your entire day. And, as I mentioned, applying The Process is actually quite a fun and joyous experience you'll actually look forward to. I do as do all my clients and students who apply it.

If I'm at home and by myself and I feel discomfort, I apply The Process with my eyes closed while reclining in a meditation chair I have in my home office. If I'm engaged in conversation with other people, say at dinner or a party, and I feel discomfort, I look away and apply The Process, or I look down and touch my fingers to my forehead like I'm deep in thought, or I excuse myself and go to the restroom to apply The Process there. You'll figure out how to do it in various situations. It's not hard and just takes some common sense and practice.

KEY POINT   You don't always have to apply The Process "in the heat of the moment."

Even though it ultimately becomes quick and easy to apply The Process, there will still be times when you'll decide it's not convenient or possible to do it in the heat of the moment when the discomfort gets naturally triggered. That's fine. If that happens, you have two choices:

1. Defer it and apply The Process later, when it is convenient, by simply replaying the trigger scene in Consciousness, recreating the feelings of discomfort and applying The Process to them then.

2. Ignore the opportunity to reclaim power and know that it will return another day.

There's an additional application of The Process I want to share with you that you're going to love. Sometimes, when you feel discomfort, you just feel a vague, unfocused sense of discomfort. At other times, something gets popped into your hologram which causes you discomfort but also sets off a very specific chain reaction of responses in your mind: "Oh no, if this happens, that will happen, then this, then that, then that, then . . . Ahhhhhhh!" And you find yourself imagining a *disaster* being the ultimate outcome of the chain of events.

For example, as I mentioned in the Introduction, after having had the experience of crashing and burning financially once, when I created the illusion of money appearing to disappear from my accounts again many years later, I created a chain reaction in my mind like this: "If money keeps pouring out like this with no income, I'm going to go through all my cash reserves. Then I'll end up losing my dream home, having to pull the kids out of private school, and having to fire my loyal employees. I'll be shamed in our community and with our friends, shamed with my father and shamed among my writing, speaking, and teaching peers, I'll go into a deep depression I'll never recover from. . . ."

If you experience a chain reaction of *loss* like that, or you find yourself experiencing deep fear about any specific *disastrous event* taking place, even if there isn't a long chain of events preceding it, imagine the entire disaster scenario playing out *in Consciousness*. Take it through to its logical and *disastrous* conclusion. Then, when you experience the tremendous discomfort that results, apply The Process to it. By doing that, you'll support your Phase 2 journey in three ways:

1. You'll reclaim power from a gigantic egg or interlinked series of eggs.

2. Once the eggs are drained, the discomfort will be gone *permanently.*

3. By experiencing the *disaster* in Consciousness, there's no need for you to pop it into your hologram and experience it in more tangible form.

| KEY POINT | **Until you reclaim power from an egg/pattern, it will continue** |

to *appear* real, act real, and have power over you.

It's very important to understand that having an intellectual *understanding* that something isn't real, is made up, is a creation of your Consciousness, and reclaiming power from it are very different things. That's why so many Phase 1 self-help, personal growth, success, and metaphysical techniques ultimately fail. Understanding isn't enough. Using techniques that attempt to manipulate the holographic illusion doesn't work either. You must actually reclaim power from limiting patterns in The Field in order to collapse them. While there may be another technique I'm unaware of, I know of no technique other than The Process that actually allows you to reclaim power from your Phase 1 limited creations.

The Process is the closest thing to a miracle I've ever experienced while playing The Human Game. If you commit yourself, patterns that have plagued you, caused you pain, and limited your finances and the flow of abundance to you will simply disappear from your hologram. Things that used to scare you to death will make you laugh. Things that used to automatically trigger you into anger, fear, embarrassment, frustration, feeling weak, or small, will simply be gone—poof—and you'll feel joyfulness, peace, and power instead. It's truly remarkable. Plus, as you'll soon see, you'll naturally open up to the infinite power, wisdom, and abundance that's your natural state.

I was speaking with my wife, Cecily, about this yesterday. She used to run a pattern where she'd create tremendous discomfort she called "emotional storms" that would scoop her up, spin her around, and she'd feel powerless to do anything about them. "I just did my best to survive it and wait it out since I knew it would blow over in an hour or a couple of days," she said. After entering Phase 2 and having The Process on her tool belt, whenever a storm came, she wasn't helpless. She wasn't at the mercy of the storm. She didn't need to wait it out. She just applied The Process and reclaimed the power from it. She knows that as she reclaims more and more power, the storms will come less and less, then stop altogether.

In Phase 2, discomfort is just a flashing red sign that says, "There's power here! There's power here! Come get me! Come get me!" So you go get the power and magic happens!

KEY POINT   **In Phase 1, you want to make** *bad feelings* **go away. In Phase 2, you say "bring them on" so you can reclaim your power from the limiting eggs you installed in The Field.**

Even though there are five more chapters in this book and our journey together isn't over, I'd like to suggest that you take some time as soon as possible to get your feet wet by applying The Process.

You may be feeling discomfort about something this very minute—a *bill, problem, or issue*. Or maybe something new will get popped into your hologram later today or tomorrow. The sooner you start applying it, getting comfortable with it, and customizing the guidelines I gave you for your unique situation, the more effective it will be for you and the more power you'll reclaim.

We'll be discussing The Process again in the chapters that follow, but it's now time to discuss the other two treasure hunting tools you'll use to play in Phase 2 of The Human Game.

Tool 3: The Mini-Process

As you move into Phase 2 of The Human Game, you'll notice two scenarios unfolding related to money and finances (and other creations unrelated to money):

1. Experiences that cause you to feel discomfort
2. Experiences that don't cause you to feel discomfort but point the way to limiting eggs in The Field

When you feel discomfort, you apply The Process. When you don't feel discomfort but you see limitation at work, you apply the Mini-Process. To distinguish between the two, if you look at your checking account statement and feel uncomfortable because the balance seems so low, you apply The Process to it. However, if you see your checking account statement, look at the balance, and you *don't* feel uncomfortable (because it seems "big" or "enough" or however you'd label it), you apply the Mini-Process. Why? Because your checking account isn't real, the deposit and withdrawal numbers on the statement aren't real, and the balance isn't real, so you know you're looking at a limited creation, an illusion. You want to take the opportunity to reclaim your power from it and reaffirm what's True to support you in busting loose from The Money Game.

| KEY POINT | In Phase 1, you told yourself over and over, ad infinitum, "money is real, the checking account is real, the numbers are real, The Money Game is real." In Phase 2, you reverse the process and repeat to yourself over and over, "It's an illusion, it's an illusion, I'm creating it, I'm creating it," as you reclaim your power from it.

The Mini-Process is the same as The Process except you don't dive into the discomfort as step one because there isn't any discomfort there. So, you simply follow the remaining steps:

1. "I am _____ creating this." (Fill in the blank with the description you chose.)

2. "It's not real." (Really feel the meaning of the words.)

3. "It's completely made up." (Really feel the meaning of the words.)

4. "It's a creation of *my* Consciousness." (Really feel the meaning of the words.)

5. "I reclaim my power from this creation NOW."

6. "As I reclaim the power, I feel it coming back to me." (Feel it.)

7. "I feel it surging through me." (Really feel it surging.)

8. "As I feel the surge, I feel myself expanding more and more and expressing more and more of who I really am in my Human Experience. I am _____." (Insert the description you chose.)

9. Fully appreciate how amazing you had to be to create this and convince yourself it was real, how amazing the creation was, and how beautifully it served you in Phase 1.

If you're short of time or are looking at numerous limited creations simultaneously, you can abbreviate this from time to time by only doing steps 1 through 5. However, the more you do, the faster you'll accelerate through Phase 2 and toward busting loose from The Money Game. The key structural component here is to look at all limiting illusions in your hologram (especially the financial ones), tell The Truth about them, and reclaim your power.

Tool 5: Empowering Vocabulary and Self-Talk

As part of The Money Game, we have numerous ideas, concepts, and words that are used to reinforce the illusion of financial limitation. To complement the use of Appreciation, The Process, and the Mini-Process in Phase 2, you want to modify your vocabulary and self-talk to support your ever-growing expansion and opening to your natural state of Infinite Abundance.

Therefore, you want to watch your conversation and self-talk carefully and transform all ideas, concepts, and words like the following by replacing them with a Phase 2 alternative as suggested next—feeling the Truth and meaning of the new wording as much as you possibly can as you do it:

Phase 1 Term	Phase 2 Replacement
Cost	Request for appreciation
The Bill	The request for appreciation
Expense	Expression of appreciation
Overhead	Fixed monthly expressions of appreciation
Price	Requested expression of appreciation
How Much?	What is the requested appreciation for this creation?
Payment	Expression of appreciation

On and on. You get the idea. Just like with applying The Process, the Phase 2 alternative wording may feel empty or fake at first, but it will become more and more real the more you use it and the deeper you move into Phase 2.

Let's get real for a minute. If you go into a store, bank, or restaurant, or speak to a friend or spouse who knows nothing about Phase 2 or busting loose from The Money Game, they'll think you're nuts if you use Phase 2 phrases like I suggested. That's where self-talk comes in. If you're in a situation where you must use Phase 1 wording when speaking to someone else, then simultaneously remind yourself of The Truth and feel The Truth in your own thoughts and feelings. This may seem minor or nit-picky, but in Phase 2, we're all about draining the power out of financially limiting eggs—not adding more power to them or keeping the status quo. Changing your vocabulary and self-talk supports that goal beautifully.

When you apply the four treasure hunting tools—Appreciation, The Process, the Mini-Process, and Empowering Vocabulary and Self-Talk, day in and day out, amazing things start to happen. To discover what applying the tools looks like, exactly how to apply them on a daily basis, and what to expect as you apply them on your journey toward busting loose from The Money Game, turn the page to continue with Chapter 11.

Busting Loose

As soon as you trust yourself, you will know how to live.[1]
—Johann Wolfgang Von Goethe,
Poet and Dramatist (1749–1832)

Now, we've come a long way together, haven't we? You now understand how Phase 1 and Phase 2 of The Human Game work. You understand the science underlying my model and the mechanics of how you create everything you experience in the total immersion movie you call life. You also have all the treasure hunting tools you need to bust loose from The Money Game.

In this chapter you're going to discover how to combine and use the four treasure hunting tools in your daily life. I'm also going to start discussing what to expect as you begin using them. Then, in Chapter 12, I'll share numerous stories from my own life and the lives of clients and students to illustrate what Phase 2 living can look and feel like (but remember that you'll custom design your own Phase 2 experiences).

KEY POINT   In Phase 2, nothing has any significance, importance, meaning, stability, or solidity except to the extent to which it supports you in using the four treasure hunting tools.

In Phase 1 of The Human Game, your focus was on what appeared to be outside of you. In Phase 2, the focus shifts to what's going on *inside* of you. In Phase 1, it was all about hiding your power, limiting yourself, and convincing yourself you're the exact opposite of who you really are. In Phase 2, it's all about reclaiming power, remembering who you are, reaffirming The Truth, expanding, dramatically increasing your levels of appreciation, and un-limiting yourself. That's what I call the Phase 2 work.

In Phase 1, what's happening in your hologram is very important to you. In Phase 1, the details matter. In Phase 2, the details are irrelevant. Why? Because they're all being created by your Expanded Self for the sole purpose of supporting you in doing the Phase 2 work. In Phase 2, it doesn't matter if you quit a job or keep it, continue a romantic relationship or end it, go left or right at a fork in the road, make or lose money, fight or have joyous times with your family. It doesn't matter if your career thrives or dives. It doesn't matter what your checking account balance or net worth is (or how they change).

The story line doesn't matter. The only thing that matters is how the story line gives you opportunities to use the treasure hunting tools and do the Phase 2 work. The goal in Phase 2 is to get you to the point where you can play The Human Game without any limits or restrictions. Because that treasure is so precious and goes beyond anything you can imagine to be possible for yourself right now, everything else pales in comparison.

This concept is tricky. On the surface, it's easily understandable from a logical perspective. However, there are subtleties to it that don't become clear until you've had numerous Phase 2 experiences that *show you* the Truthfulness of it. For now, just allow the seeds to be planted. They'll be watered and nurtured and grow tall at a later date.

As you move into Phase 2, your Expanded Self will create patterns in The Field, energize them with tremendous power, and pop them into your hologram to give you opportunities to apply the four treasure hunting tools and bust loose from The Money Game. In Phase 1 of The Human Game, you were taught to be proactive, go out there and make things happen, take massive action, set goals and achieve them, get the job done. That pattern was so strongly installed within me that it took me nine months to reclaim the power and collapse it.

In Phase 2, it's the exact opposite. In Phase 2 you live in what I call *reactive mode*. You wake up in the morning and wait to see what gets popped into your hologram and what you feel motivated or inspired to do. When something pops in, you respond to it. When you feel motivated or inspired to do something, you do it. You do that all day long. Then you go to bed at night, wake up the next morning, and do it again. In Phase 2, there are no goals, agendas, or desired outcomes. There are no one-year plans, five-year plans, or ten-year plans. You squeeze your focus way back and take life one moment at a time.

It's like you're a handyman. When you're a handyman, you wait for someone to call with projects for you to complete. When you're called, you go to the home or office and consider what needs to be done. You then choose a tool from your tool belt or truck and do what needs to be done. When you're done with one tool and one project, you choose another tool to complete another project, always using the right tool for the job. Sometimes you use a screw-driver, sometimes a paintbrush, sometimes a drill or saw. Figure 11.1 shows the tools you have on your Phase 2 tool belt.

As you're taking life one moment at a time and living in reactive mode, if an experience gets popped into your hologram that causes you discomfort, you pull The Process tool from your belt and use it. If something gets popped into your hologram that doesn't cause you discomfort but points to a limiting egg in The Field (like

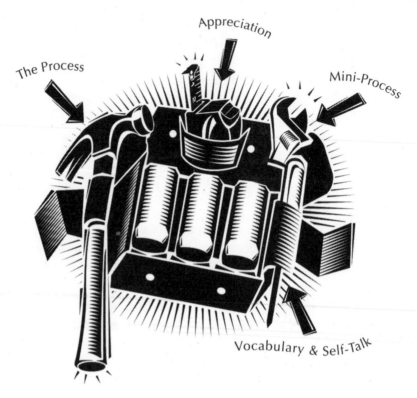

FIGURE 11.1   Your Phase 2 tool belt.

a bank statement, financial statement, monthly report on the value of your stock portfolio, bill, etc.), you pull the Mini-Process tool from your belt and use it. If you find yourself thinking or speaking with limited Phase 1 language, you pull your Empowering Vocabulary and Self-Talk tool from your belt and use it. Every opportunity you get, you pull the Appreciation tool from your belt and appreciate the magnificence of your creations, yourself as the Creator of everything you experience, and The Human Game itself.

If you have a decision to make in the course of a day, you do what you feel motivated or inspired to do, trusting it's the perfect choice since you're being guided every step of the way by your Expanded Self. If you have discomfort about the decision, you apply The Process to the discomfort and continue applying it until you have no discomfort about the decision when you focus on it. Then, from that expanded state, you do what you feel motivated or inspired to do, trusting it's the perfect choice.

KEY POINT **Your Expanded Self is driving the bus in Phase 2. You can't make a mistake, mess anything up, or blow it. You just trust your Expanded Self and flow with what you feel inspired or motivated to do, moment to moment.**

In Phase 1, you convinced yourself there is power in the hologram, that you, the Persona, was driving the bus, and that the burden and responsibility for getting things done was on your shoulders. In Phase 2, you completely let go of that. You surrender into the Phase 2 game and allow your Expanded Self to guide you. If anxiousness, anxiety, or worry comes up as you let go, or as you consider letting go, you apply The Process to it. You were never in control in Phase 1 anyway. There never was any power in the hologram. It was all an illusion. Your Expanded Self was always in control and had the power, so by letting go and trusting in Phase 2, you're just affirming The Truth and living from it.

You don't have to go looking for eggs to reclaim power from. You just follow the lead of your Expanded Self who will take you to them. As we discussed, your Expanded Self knows where the eggs with the most power are hidden. Your Expanded Self knows where to put the dynamite charges in the limited "building" you constructed in Phase 1 so you can collapse it when you're ready. As we also discussed, to continue the metaphor of demolishing a building, you don't have to put a dynamite charge on every brick in the building, just on the key foundational bricks that support the structure of your illusion.

Applying The Process to play the Phase 2 game requires an enormous amount of courage, patience, discipline, commitment, and diligence. Why? Because as I explained in Chapter 10, your

Expanded Self will lead you to find and open eggs that stimulate incredibly intense feelings of discomfort within you. In Phase 1 of The Human Game, you ran away from discomfort like that or tried to repress it, muffle it, or make it go away. In Phase 2, you dive into the heart of it, and it takes tremendous courage, discipline, and commitment to do that, maintain the "bring it on" attitude and continue applying The Process to the discomfort day after day, even when you feel like giving up.

KEY POINT   **As you do the Phase 2 work, you must always remember the treasure that awaits you at the end of the journey. It's worth it!**

Applying The Process also requires you to be absolutely realistic in terms of how much you can do and how fast you can do it. Once you get a taste of the power of the treasure hunting tools, you may want to apply The Process and reclaim power from everything in your life—all at once—and you may also want everything to change in your hologram—all at once—and neither choice is supportive. Remember, the goal is *not* to instantaneously reclaim all your power and transform your hologram in one fell swoop. Your Expanded Self is going to lead you to the eggs with the most power in them and by design support you in reclaiming power through many applications of The Process over time until the foundational eggs have been fully drained. In some cases, I've drained eggs in days or weeks. With other eggs, it took months, a year, or even more. Your Expanded Self will also support you in fully appreciating those creations and yourself as the Creator of them. As you move more deeply into Phase 2, the Appreciation tool becomes more and more important, as you'll see.

KEY POINT   **In Phase 1, you're taught "fast is better." In Phase 2, speed is irrelevant. It's the ultimate goal of playing The**

Human Game without limits or restrictions you're after. The timetable has no importance and will be absolutely perfect for you, no matter how long it takes.

There will also be times when you'll feel discomfort, you'll apply The Process and feel joyous and expanded when you come out the other end. Then, a few seconds, minutes, or hours later, you'll find yourself feeling what appears to be the exact same thing "coming back" again. It may feel the same but it never is. It's never a boomerang. It's always something new. Whenever you apply The Process to reclaim power, you reclaim power. You're not kidding yourself or pretending. It's real, even if you don't always feel different immediately afterward (and many times you will). Each time you apply The Process, you change, you move into a more expanded state of Consciousness, and everything is different for you. If the same thing appears to be cycling back, it's more power from the same egg but it's different power. Welcome the discomfort, dive in, apply The Process and take the power back.

| KEY POINT | Once you reclaim power, it's yours again. You can't lose it. |

Once you expand, you stay expanded. You don't ever shrink or slide backward.

In Phase 2, you reclaim power to reclaim power, and where it goes it goes. You don't reclaim power to change, fix, or improve your hologram. This is such a critical point to get and it will be challenging for you at the start. You don't reclaim power to make something *bad* go away or something *good* show up or increase in quantity. You don't reclaim power to triple the sales of your business, double your income, get out of debt, increase the productivity of your employees, get a promotion, feel better, or produce *any* specific result. You detach from all agendas and investments in results and outcomes. I realize this is easier said than done but you'll open into this mind-set naturally as you do the Phase 2 work over time. It will just happen.

It can be extremely tempting, when something *bad* appears to happen with cash flow, your business, or finances to apply The Process, then start looking at your hologram to see if something changed *as a result*. But that doesn't support you in busting loose from The Money Game. This gets tricky, it's subtle, and there's quicksand here you want to avoid, so please listen closely. If you want to change, fix, or improve something in your hologram, what are you doing? Judging it! You're saying "I don't like this." As we discussed, judgment is the glue that keeps the Phase 1 illusions locked in place, so if you judge a creation, what happens? You keep strengthening the glue that's keeping that creation in your hologram. In effect, you keep saying, "This is real! This is real!" And the illusion *must* therefore stay locked in place. In Phase 2, your goal is to reclaim power from the eggs, not feed them.

KEY POINT You can't judge a creation, reclaim power from it, and collapse its pattern simultaneously. It's simply not possible.

Let's go more deeply into this key concept. In Phase 1, there's the illusion of a cause and effect relationship between actions and results. We convince ourselves "If I do x and y I'll get z." In Truth, there's no such relationship *from within the hologram*. That is, there's no cause *in the hologram* that creates an effect *in the hologram*. The True cause is always outside the hologram. The True cause is always your Consciousness, a pattern in The Field, and your power.

If you apply The Process then look for a change in your hologram *as a result*, what are you doing? You're looking for proof of The Truth and you're therefore energizing the belief, "I'm not sure The Truth is true." You're looking at a creation and saying, "Hey you, *bad* creation, go away and then I'll believe" or "Hey you, *good* creation, come in and then I'll believe." And when you do that, nothing can change in your hologram and you can't reclaim power or expand.

Why? Because you're continuing to feed power into your limitation eggs. Do you see that? If not, you will if you make the choice to leap into Phase 2 and do the work for a while. In Phase 2, your goal is to see and really "get" that nothing in the hologram is real and YOU have all the power. The goal is *not* to strengthen the illusion.

When I've shared this with clients and students throughout the world, they all understand the concept, but some say, "I don't like my present situation. That's why I want to bust loose from The Money Game. Of course I want to change my hologram. Of course I want to fix it. Of course I want to improve it. How am I supposed to reconcile the conflict here?" Did that thought cross your mind, too? Here's my answer: You can't fix, change, or improve an illusion. It's not real. There's nothing to fix, change, or improve. It's all smoke and mirrors.

Look at this from another angle. Suppose you try to reclaim power with an agenda: "I want to reclaim power so I can double my income." Or, "I want to reclaim power so I can wipe out my debt." Or, "I want to reclaim power so I can double sales for my business." Suppose you succeeded in creating your desired result. All you're doing is trading one illusion for another. All you're doing is trading one *limited* creation for another *limited* creation. You don't want to do that. You want to bust loose from The Money Game *entirely*. You want to reach the point where you can play The Human Game without any restrictions or limits at all. As long as you want to change, fix, or improve your hologram, as long as you have an agenda, goal, or outcome, you're feeding the limited reality of the illusion and adding power to the very eggs you want to drain to bust loose.

Plus, consider this as it relates to why you don't want to try to change, fix, or improve your hologram. Every single creation you pop into your hologram is an absolute miracle. There's nothing there. It's all smoke and mirrors. Yet it appears absolutely real because of how talented and powerful a Creator you are. Having $50,000 in the bank isn't better than having $500 in the bank. Being a millionaire isn't better than being broke or $25,000 in debt.

ɔm The Money Game and opening up to the Infi-
that's your natural state isn't better than playing
and being locked into financial limitation.

ɪnose creations are all *different*, but they're are all equal creations and equally magnificent creations when viewed from the
expanded perspective of the Real You. Is a character in a movie who
has $5 to his name worse off than another character who has tens of
millions to his name? No. Neither character is real. They're all made
up as are the numbers they appear to have to their names. It's the
same with the illusions in your hologram.

All creations are perfect exactly as they are. They wouldn't be
in your hologram if there wasn't a pattern in The Field that got
energized. There wouldn't be a pattern in The Field if your
Expanded Self didn't put one there—intentionally, based on
a brilliant plan—to support you perfectly on your journey, no
matter what definition, label, or judgment you might apply to the
creation.

The only reason certain creations appear *better* to you is
because you're locked into a Phase 1 perspective where you're
judging them, making up stories about them, and convincing
yourself the stories are real. I realize this may be tough to accept
right now, but it's The Truth and that's what you created me to
share with you. As I mentioned, all the concepts I've been sharing with you here will become more and more real as you reclaim
more and more power and expand more and more while doing the
Phase 2 work.

Your hologram *will change* as you do the Phase 2 work. You could
look at those changes and judge them as *better*. However, The Truth
is, your life doesn't get *better*. It just gets *different* and the differences
allow you to play different games for the pure pleasure of playing
them. When you reclaim enough power and regain enough of your
Infinite Wisdom to be able to see this—really see it—and "get it" at
a very deep and profound level (which you will if you commit to
playing the Phase 2 game), that's the signal you're about to bust
loose from The Money Game!

KEY POINT When you get to the point in Phase 2 where you can truly say "I want to create X" from the place of simply wanting to experience the pure joy of playing with that creation, you can create it. However, if you're not fully appreciating what you've already created, or there's the slightest bit of judgment or Phase 1 energy in the "wish" to create something, it will *not* pop into your hologram.

This is subtle but so very important and a major hurdle you'll have to jump if you commit to the Phase 2 game. If you're like I was and like many of my students and clients have been, despite this knowledge, you may be tempted on many occasions to apply The Process with an agenda of wanting to change, fix, or improve your hologram—and you may give in to that temptation. If that happens, so be it. It's not a big deal. As I explained, you can't mess up your hologram or make a mistake in Phase 2. However, if you try to reclaim power with an agenda, or you try to change, fix, or improve your hologram, you'll see it simply doesn't work. Then, as you continue to do the Phase 2 work and expand, the desire to fix, change, or improve your hologram will ultimately fall away—naturally.

KEY POINT If you want to bust loose from The Money Game, you don't care what the illusions look like in your hologram along the way. You just go with the flow and apply your four treasure hunting tools as the opportunities arise.

Other clients and students say to me, "That *sounds* great, but it's just not practical for me. I own my own business, and I have to focus on the numbers, goals, and outcomes." Or, "I have a job where my boss expects me to set and achieve goals on a regular basis." Or, "I have overhead and a family to feed. I can't afford to be so la-dee-da and frivolous." If thoughts like that crossed your mind, take a deep breath and allow me to remind you of several Truths that will get more and more real for you as you expand and move more deeply into Phase 2 of The Human Game. In the examples I just gave:

- There is no business.
- There are no numbers.
- There are no goals or outcomes.
- There is no job.
- There is no boss.
- There is no overhead or family to feed.

It's all made up. It's all just a creation of your Consciousness. There's no power outside of you—not in anyone, not in anything. *You* have all the power and your Expanded Self will use it brilliantly in Phase 2—with your job, business, boss, family, and everything else—to support you in doing the Phase 2 work and busting loose from The Money Game.

Whether you own your own business, work for someone else, are unemployed, single, married with children, or whatever your situation is, you can still take life one moment at a time, still live in reactive mode, and still use the treasure hunting tools to bust loose from The Money Game without agenda, goals, or an investment in specific outcomes or results. I do it every day and have been for years even though I own multiple businesses, am married, and have two young children. I'll show you exactly how I do it in the next chapter, and offer additional guidelines you can follow. There's absolutely nothing unique about me in this respect.

I'd now like to chat with you about what to expect as you begin using the four treasure hunting tools on your journey deep into the heart of Phase 2. Here's a brief summary, then we'll discuss each point in detail.

What to Expect in Phase 2

1. Expect to be uncomfortable.
2. Expect "weird things" to happen.
3. Expect to have *all* your core beliefs challenged.
4. Expect to feel confused, frustrated, overwhelmed, and disoriented at times.

1. Expect to Be Uncomfortable

The greatest amount of power is hidden where you feel the most discomfort. Therefore, to reclaim power, you must be uncomfortable a lot of the time, especially at the start of your Phase 2 journey. That's just the way it is. In fact, you'll know the moment you actually enter Phase 2 because one or more things will be created and popped into your hologram that are unusual and intense and cause you a great deal of discomfort. Discomfort is the name of the game in Phase 2. It's a great gift for the reasons you now understand.

In Phase 1, the knee-jerk reaction to tremendous discomfort is something like this:

"I hate this."

"Get me out of here."

"Why is this happening to me?"

"I can't handle this right now."

"Go away!"

. . . all of which support the Phase 1 goal of limitation and convincing yourself you're the exact opposite of who you really are. In Phase 2, the opportunity you give yourself is to apply The Process, reclaim your power from those creations, and march ever closer to the Busting Loose Point.

2. Expect Weird Things to Happen

Three primary goals for Phase 2 of The Human Game are:

1. Reclaiming power.
2. Showing yourself how brilliantly you fooled yourself in Phase 1.
3. Supporting yourself in remembering who you really are, how powerful you really are, and that you're creating everything you experience, down to the smallest detail.

To achieve those goals, experiences must be created that seem "weird" to you. What does "weird" really mean anyway? A definition I recently saw in a dictionary is: "Of a strikingly odd or unusual character; strange." If you're an Infinite Being who convinced yourself you're the exact opposite of who you really are, and you suddenly started showing yourself who you really are and how powerful you really are, don't you think what you'll see must appear strange, strikingly odd, or of an unusual character from a Phase 1 perspective? You bet! As far as I'm concerned from personal experience in my own life and with thousands of clients and students worldwide, the weirder it appears the greater the opportunity for expansion you create for yourself. In the next chapter, I'll be sharing numerous stories of just how weird things can appear.

The other thing you'll notice is that things may get so weird you'll wonder if they really happened or you just imagined them. My experience in my own life and with clients has been that in the early part of Phase 2, whenever you have a major experience of The Truth, seeing how powerful you really are, and the degree to which you really do create and control everything that's happening to you, it has a surreal aspect to it. If you experience it that way, it will change over time.

3. Expect to Have All Your Core Beliefs Challenged

As you know, each limiting pattern in The Field has one or more beliefs inside it. None of them are true. They're all made up. Therefore, if you're going to bust loose from The Money Game, every single one of your core money beliefs, the beliefs that are keeping you locked into limitation in the illusion will be pushed, poked, prodded, and ultimately collapsed. That must happen.

| **KEY POINT** | You can't simultaneously continue believing what you |

convinced yourself was true in Phase 1 and bust loose from The Money Game. It's not possible. They're mutually exclusive activities.

4. Expect to Feel Confused, Frustrated, Overwhelmed, and Disoriented at Times

If you're going to be experiencing a lot of discomfort in Phase 2, seeing a lot of weird things, and if everything you thought was true gets challenged to its very core, do you think you might feel confused, frustrated, overwhelmed, and disoriented at times?

Of course!

I laugh about it now, but there were many times in my first year of doing the Phase 2 work when I looked up to the sky and said to my Expanded Self, "You've overestimated my ability to deal with this. This is too much. I can't handle it. I need a break. Please make it stop or let me plateau for a while."

The good news is those feelings qualify as discomfort, right? So if you feel confused, apply The Process to it. If you feel frustrated, apply The Process to it. If you feel overwhelmed, apply The Process to it. If you feel disoriented, apply The Process to it. When you come out the other end after applying The Process and you're immersed in the Infinite Energy, you won't feel any of those things. You'll be in an expanded state—until your Expanded Self leads you to another egg or back to an "old" egg that still has power in it.

KEY POINT **Your Expanded Self knows you better than you could ever possibly know yourself. He or She never gives you more than He or She knows you can handle. Even if you think you're overwhelmed or past your limit, you're not and you *can* handle it. Just apply The Process with the absolute certainty that you're going to be just fine.**

In Chapter 6, I explained that other people, playing the roles of actors in your total immersion movie, serve three purposes in your hologram:

1. Reflect something back you're thinking or feeling about yourself or a belief you've energized.
2. Share supportive knowledge, wisdom, or insight with you.
3. Set something in motion to support you on your journey.

Therefore, your Expanded Self will be handing scripts to the actors in your life and asking them to say and do all kinds of things to support you in doing the Phase 2 work. Therefore, expect to see people saying and doing all kinds of weird things, inconsistent things, perhaps out-of-character things—all to support you on your Phase 2 journey. For example, as she deepened her Phase 2 work, one of my clients, a woman we'll call Nancy, created what she called her "Christmas Eve from Hell," where every single member of her extended family acted completely crazy, out of character, and in ways she'd *never* seen them act before. That creation gave her numerous opportunities to do the Phase 2 work.

You may feel tempted to try to figure out why such things are happening or which of the three purposes the words and actions of the actors in your movie are supporting. Let go of the desire to figure things out. If your Expanded Self wants you to benefit from a reflection, knowledge, wisdom, insight, or something being set in motion by an actor in your hologram, He or She will make it obvious and crystal clear to you. You won't need to go digging for it or racking your *brain* for answers. You just keep using your four treasure hunting tools, reclaiming power, and expanding the Consciousness with which you play The Human Game. The rest takes care of itself.

| KEY POINT | Phase 2 is *not* about figuring things out, logic, or intellect. |

It's about feelings and direct experiences. *Understanding* is the booby prize in Phase 2.

This is one of the things I appreciate most about Phase 2. In Phase 1, I tried to live my life exclusively from logic and intellect. It was a very stressful way to live, it exhausted me, and it was ultimately a strategy that didn't work (since nothing can be allowed to *work* consistently in Phase 1). I found it incredibly relaxing and joyful to let go of intellect, logic, figuring things out, and just follow my feelings. You will too.

As I mentioned earlier, a big part of Phase 2 of The Human Game is appreciating what a miraculous job you did of fooling yourself into thinking the illusion was real and you were the exact opposite of who you really are. Therefore, as you're taken to eggs to reclaim the power from them, your Expanded Self will also take you on a tour of exactly how you pulled that miracle off. As you come out the other end after applying The Process, you'll find yourself frequently saying something like this to yourself, "So that's how I did it! How did I ever buy into that? Amazing!"

I can't tell you exactly what Phase 2 or the Busting Loose Process will look like for you. It's different for everybody. But your

knows how to bust you loose as a unique Infinite
a unique Human Game. What I can absolutely guar-
..ce you is if you have the courage, persistence, commitment, and
discipline to do the Phase 2 work and stick with it—even when it
feels scary, uncomfortable, and awkward—you'll come to love it.
And the transformations you ultimately see in your hologram and
internal experience will blow your mind.

I want to make two critical points before we close this chapter.
First, be gentle and patient with yourself as you do the Phase 2
work. You don't have to become a master at using the treasure
hunting tools overnight. If you find yourself saying things like this
to yourself:

"I'm just not doing it right."

"I just had the opportunity to reclaim 100 ounces of power and
I only got 20. Shit!"

"I'm never going to able to do this."

"I just don't have what it takes to stick it out."

"No matter how hard I work or try, it's just not working for me."

"I can't do it!"

Recognize the voices as old limiting creations that served you well
in Phase 1 but don't serve you any longer. Apply The Process to
them. You just do what you can do and trust that everything is working out perfectly, no matter what's happening or what it looks like.
You're *always* doing it perfectly, no matter what it looks like!

KEY POINT **Never underestimate what it
took to convince yourself the
illusion was real and you were the exact opposite of
who you really are.**

For however many years you've been alive, you've used every
ounce of power, creativity, inventiveness, cleverness, and trickiness
you had as an Infinite Being to convince yourself the illusion was

real and you were the exact opposite of who you really are. You beat yourself over the head unmercifully, "The physical world is real, the physical world is real, money is real, money is real, my checking account is real, my checking account is real, I really am limited, I really am limited," until you were absolutely convinced. You were relentless to take yourself from infinite to finite. Now you must reverse all of that and take yourself from finite back into infinite. It's going to take time, energy, effort, and discipline. Be prepared for that and give yourself a break or apply The Process if you judge yourself for being too slow, or if it feels like there's too much to do, or whatever else comes up for you.

In short, in Phase 2 you:

- Follow the lead of your Expanded Self.
- Wait to see what pops into your hologram or what you feel inspired to do.
- Pull the tools off your tool belt and patiently use them as you feel so moved to respond to what pops in—without agenda or wanting to fix, change, or improve your hologram.

After you do that, day in and day out, you'll wake up one morning and notice something has changed in your hologram. Maybe something that used to drive you crazy now makes you laugh. Maybe someone who always appeared to be a jerk to you suddenly starts appearing to be kind and supportive. Maybe money starts *showing up* from unexpected places. One thing will change. Then something else. Then something else. Then the rate and quantity of change will start to accelerate into what I call "miraculous territory." But it all comes from the patient, persistent, and detached application of the treasure hunting tools on a daily basis.

KEY POINT You don't proactively make things happen or "manifest results" in Phase 2. You simply do the Phase 2 work and as you do it, more and more clouds get

dissolved and more and more of the sun of who you really are starts shining in. When that happens, your hologram changes on its own—naturally—in amazing ways.

To me, Phase 1 was exhausting. It was so complicated. There were so many choices and options, so much work to do, so many things to make happen, so many details to analyze, process, and manage to prosper. My levels of joyfulness, peace, and satisfaction soared off the charts as I moved more deeply into Phase 2 (and they continue to rise). You'll create the same dynamic for yourself.

One of the other things I love and appreciate so much about the Phase 2 game is it's so simple! You only have four tools on your tool belt, and it's obvious when to use each one. You live in reactive mode, wait to see what you feel motivated or inspired to do and what pops into your hologram. Then you simply trust your Expanded Self and do what you feel motivated to do or pull out the right tool for the job and use it. You do that day after day, and as you reclaim your power, you expand in your wisdom and abundance. Then, one day, you reach the Busting Loose Point where you've reclaimed enough power, affirmed The Truth enough, and appreciated enough that you bust loose and your hologram transforms—naturally and without effort— in ways you can't even imagine right now. I'll be going into great detail on what the Busting Loose Point looks like in Chapter 13.

| KEY POINT | **Everything you've discovered so far will get more and more real and your understanding of its Truth will deepen as you continue to reclaim power and expand your Consciousness.** |

I'd now like to share a variety of mind-blowing stories from my life, my clients, and my students to illustrate what Phase 2 life *can* look like. When you're ready to hear those stories, turn the page and continue on to Chapter 12.

Postcards from the Road

History is a set of lies agreed upon.[1]

—Napoleon Bonaparte

There are two ways to live your life. One is as though nothing is a miracle. The other is as though everything is a miracle.[2]

—Albert Einstein

A s you prepare to enter Phase 2 of The Human Game, it can be very supportive to hear specific stories about what the journey has looked like for other people. However, you must look at those stories from a clear perspective. In Phase 1, there's a tendency to look at what happens to one person and create a belief that says, "That's how it is and how it will be for me, too." We've also been given a belief in Phase 1 that a powerful success strategy is to model the behavior of other people, that if you do what they do, the way they do it, you can produce similar results. That belief is particularly seductive if we have great respect for the person being modeled and really want what he or she appears to have.

Neither belief is supportive to you in Phase 2. Everything I share from my life was custom designed to support me as a unique Infinite Being in playing The Human Game in unique ways with unique eggs that were placed in The Field just for me by my Expanded Self. Everything I share about the journeys of my family, clients, and students was custom designed to support them as unique Infinite Beings playing The Human Game in unique ways with unique eggs that were placed in The Field just for them—by *their* Expanded Selves.

| KEY POINT | There's absolutely no relation-ship between what happens for |

you in Phase 2 and what happens for *someone else.*

I could share thousands of Phase 2 stories with you from my life and the lives of my family, students, and clients. That's not necessary nor would it ultimately be supportive to you. I do want to share several stories to illustrate what the "expect to be uncomfortable," and "expect weird things" aspects of Phase 2 *can* look like, and also several stories to show what it *can* look like when you start showing yourself who you really are, how powerful you really are, and the degree to which you really are creating everything you experience, down to the smallest detail. Some of the stories may seem big or major to you. Others may seem small or insignificant to you. They're all important and were chosen with care to clearly illustrate specific key points I want you to see.

Some of the names of the people whose stories I'm going to share have been changed at their request to protect their privacy. The stories are all true without embellishment. As you read them, please keep in mind the following dialog written by William Shakespeare between Hamlet and Horatio after Horatio saw a ghost and didn't believe it was real:

HORATIO: O day and night, but this is wondrous strange!
HAMLET: And therefore as a stranger give it welcome.
There are more things in heaven and earth, Horatio,
Than are dreamt of in your philosophy.[3]

I first want to share stories about the expect discomfort part of Phase 2, with the first story being the series of events leading up to me busting loose from The Money Game. In Chapter 1, I laid out the rules of The Money Game. In Phase 1, just like you, I convinced myself the rules of The Money Game were real and the illusion had power. I therefore created eggs with very strong beliefs in them that were the exact opposite of The Truth. As a result, I created very strong core beliefs that the following were true:

- The amount of abundance I had was accurately reflected by the balances in my accounts, my income, and the net worth number on my financial statement.
- The true source of my abundance was my business activities.
- The abundance I received from my business activities was directly proportional to how good my products and services were, how many I had to offer, how profitable each sale was, and how good I was at marketing and promoting to convince other people to buy them.

To deepen the illusion that those core beliefs were true, I created myself being involved with direct response marketing and selling products and services by mail order and on the Internet for 18 years.

Because of those core beliefs, for example, I logged into my online banking portal to check the balances in my accounts every day and watched sales figures and the other financial metrics of my businesses like a hawk. When we had *good days* where sales were strong and the balances in my accounts were growing, I was happy. If we had *bad days* when sales were weak or many bills were paid with little income coming in to compensate, I was concerned. If the trend wasn't as profitable as I wanted, I'd kick into massive proactive mode to make something happen and improve things.

I explained that in Phase 2 all your core beliefs will be challenged and then dynamited to support you in opening up to The Truth and your natural state of Infinite Abundance. As a result, when I entered Phase 2, I created the following illusions and popped them into my hologram:

- Sales for the products and services of two of my businesses dropping to nearly zero. Those businesses had previously been thriving for many years, yet in the blink of an eye, with the flip of a switch, the prosperity was turned off for no apparent reason. Sales just fell off the face of the earth.
- Having to subsidize the checking accounts for the businesses from my personal resources so the bills could be paid.
- Being unable to pay myself a salary or bonus from the businesses.
- Needing to make several expensive repairs and modifications to our home.
- A triple whammy of large overhead from my personal lifestyle, no income from the two businesses, and large outgo to subsidize the business losses, causing the cash balances in my accounts to plummet. I was in no danger because I'd piled up so much money in the preceding years, but when I projected the trend forward, I could see it ultimately leading to disaster.

How do you think I felt about those creations? I can summarize it in two words: Panic and terror!

What gift do you think I gave myself by opening up eggs that led to intense feelings like those? The opportunity to reclaim *huge* amounts of power.

So what do you think I did? I applied The Process to the discomfort all day, every day. Every time I walked around my home, which is truly my dream home, or walked outside on the grounds looking at the beautiful scenery and views, I'd imagine having to sell it if the hemorrhaging of money continued. Every time I dropped the kids off at their private school in the morning, a school they adored (as did my wife), I'd imagine being unable to pay the tuition and having to pull them out. I'd imagine the shame of having to tell my father (who bailed me out when I crashed and burned earlier by co-signing a loan for me at his bank) that I'd blown it *again*—and the shame I imagined feeling when my successful entrepreneur, author, and teacher friends and associates found out about my failure. On and on the disaster scenario extended in my imagination.

Many times a day I'd log into the online system that reported on sales for my businesses hoping to see that some money had come in. But the flow of income continued at a dribble. Many times a day I had to watch the in and out flow of money in the business checking accounts and pending payments for bills so I could be sure to make a deposit from my personal account in time to prevent checks bouncing for the two businesses.

Do you see how brilliantly I was fooling myself and reinforcing the illusion of The Money Game for myself? That's what Phase 1 is all about.

Because of all that discomfort, I was often applying The Process on and off for up to three hours a day, sometimes even longer. That's how intense it was. There were also times, as I explained in the previous chapter, when I'd be feeling intense fear or panic, I'd apply The Process, I'd end up in an expanded and joyous state, then feel the fear and panic rise again seconds or minutes later. Then I'd have to go back and apply The Process again. Or I'd get a brief reprieve until I looked at the account balances or zeroes on sales statements and got stirred up again.

I explained that one of my core beliefs was the abundance of my businesses was directly proportional to my skill as a businessman and marketer and my ability to make things happen. So, out of desperation and wanting to stop the hemorrhaging of money, I shot back into aggressive proactive mode and launched a series of marketing campaigns for my various products and services. The campaigns either fell flat or produced insufficient income to have any impact on what was looking more and more like a sinking ship.

I knew about Phase 2, intellectually. I knew everything I shared with you in the previous chapters. However, as I mentioned in Chapter 10, understanding and knowing The Truth aren't enough. I had to reclaim power from the eggs that had been limiting me. To do that, I had to open up those eggs and get really uncomfortable. And to get really uncomfortable, I had to create exactly the sorts of illusions I was experiencing.

The fear and panic ultimately turned to anger. In Phase 1, I'd created the illusion of many ups and downs and a lot of pain and struggle, both growing up and in my adult life. I also created many entrepreneurial opportunities that looked like they'd catapult my success into the stratosphere but which ended up going nowhere. I perceived those as massive teases at the time. As a result, I created a very strong belief that the Universe was against me and would take any opportunity to tease me and throw wrenches into everything I was doing just for the twisted pleasure of seeing me squirm. It sounds ridiculous, I know, but in a vintage Phase 1 creation move, I actually convinced myself it was true, and I was quite angry and resentful about it. As a result, those eggs got opened big-time, and all the discomfort associated with them started flowing out with the same kind of force as water from a fire hose.

Multiple times a day, when I looked at the balances in my various accounts and saw them shrinking, I applied The Process, then used the Mini-Process to tell The Truth about them and say to myself, "Right there where those numbers are, right there where they look so real, that's my power and my Infinite Abundance at work. I'm creating all of this from my Consciousness. It's not real!" Over and over and over, day after day after day, I reminded myself of The Truth with the same ferocity with which I convinced myself of the lies in Phase 1.

At the same time that I had almost no income coming in from the two businesses, I had high personal overhead and was using my personal funds to cover the business losses, I then created a string of expenses for major repairs or necessary modifications to our home. For example, I created the illusion of a leak in our roof and two roofing companies telling me the roof was shot and I needed to replace it—a $40,000 expense. I created the illusion of a problem with water and mold in the crawl space under our home that required the installation of a water and mold abatement system that cost $13,000. The illusion of financial pressure continued to mount.

On and on it went as I watched all my core beliefs—the beliefs that had limited me the most in Phase 1 and caused me the most pain—get pushed on. It continued for eight straight months. I did have moments of incredible joyfulness and peace, a few days here and there when things were quiet and stable, but for the most part, it was an extremely intense and uncomfortable time. But I was committed to the Phase 2 journey and busting loose, so I kept at it every day, living in reactive mode, using the four treasure hunting tools, applying The Process to everything, including the anger at my Expanded Self and the Universe, the fear of crashing and burning again, and the pain and shame it would bring.

As you might guess, applying all that time, energy, and effort to the Phase 2 work and seeing nothing change or get any *better* made me even angrier. "Come on now," I'd scream to my Expanded Self, "I'm doing the work here. You know I'm committed. It's been eight months. *Something* should be shifting by now." But nothing shifted, nor could it have shifted with all the power I still had within limiting eggs in The Field.

There were times I was ready to give up, times I questioned my sanity, times I wondered if everything about Phase 1 and Phase 2, what's real and not real, reclaiming power, Infinite power, wisdom, and abundance were true or I'd just suckered myself into some crazy new belief system. There were also times when I got so *depressed* I said to my Expanded Self, "I give up. Infinite Abundance or not, playing The Human Game without limits or restrictions or not, if this is what my life is going to be like, I don't want to play anymore. Give me a breakthrough—NOW—or get me the hell out of here. I'm done with this."

But I knew what was at stake. I knew that no matter what it took, I wanted to bust loose and be able to play The Human Game without limits and restrictions, so I kept doing the Phase 2 work, despite those Phase 1 based protestations and feelings of futility. I continued reclaiming my power from agendas and wanting to change, fix, improve the hologram or get the money flowing again. Then, after doing the Phase 2 work for a year, I began to notice some change in my hologram. I noticed the feelings of panic and worry about crashing and burning again starting to decrease, then disappearing altogether. I noticed I wasn't watching the business numbers like a hawk and wasn't *absolutely* convinced they were real anymore. I noticed I'd transitioned into making decisions about what I did as it related to work based on what would be fun for me instead of what would make me money or what was expected of me. (I'll be discussing that transition in greater detail in the next chapter.) I also noticed I was feeling much more joyous and peaceful. In fact, my wife started giving me funny looks and asking me what I'd been doing because I seemed so much happier and different with her and the kids. I hadn't discussed any of the Phase 2 work with her up to that point. I'd been doing it quietly by myself. I'll be discussing the dynamic of discussing Phase 2 with "others" in Chapter 15.

I also started noticing that I was creating people being nicer to me, more attentive, more respectful, more appreciative—friends and strangers alike. Then I started noticing I was creating people *coming to me* offering me opportunities to speak at their events. In one such event, I actually created $210,000 in two minutes. I'll be sharing the details of that story later in this chapter. I created people appearing to come to me out of the blue and unsolicited, asking if they could promote my products and services to their customers and split the profits, which, in marketing terms, is called a joint venture. I accepted several of the joint ventures and an enormous amount of appreciation was expressed to me in the form of money. Consulting and coaching clients appeared to pour in—out of nowhere. Money just kept appearing to pour in from all kinds of sources, all of which were completely unexpected. The fiscal year for my businesses actually ended with record sales and profits.

Despite what looks like lots of *good news*, please understand that record sales and profits means nothing in Phase 2, the numbers weren't real, nor did I look at them as being real or meaning any-thing at that point. The key point to get here is the illusion that abundance was popped into my hologram with zero intent, desire, or proactive effort on my part as the Persona in my total immersion movie. Most importantly, responding to all those opportunities was a relaxing, joyous, and thoroughly enjoyable experience—what I call a "lifestyle friendly experience." Many people create extremely lucrative opportunities in Phase 1 but, as we discussed, they end paying a HUGE price when they *take advantage* of them.

Through all these experiences, I was showing myself how much power I really had and giving myself a taste of what was really possi-ble in Phase 2. As I shared in the previous chapter, I'd been living in reactive mode for a long time prior to seeing those creations in my hologram. I'd set no goals and had no desired outcomes or agendas. I was just living one moment at a time, doing what I felt motivated to do, doing what was fun for me, and doing the Phase 2 work. All the changes simply unfolded as a natural outgrowth of reclaiming power and collapsing patterns in The Field. That's how Phase 2 works.

As the months passed, the intensity of my experience ultimate-ly dropped and I wasn't being hit over the head with two-by-four experiences any more. Why? Because I'd reclaimed so much power by then, and that kind of intensity was no longer needed. However, I still presented myself with many opportunities to do the Phase 2 work every day. I continued to do the work, to expand, to open up more and more into who I really am, and I continued to witness many amazing and inspiring creations being popped into my holo-gram without any intent or action on my part.

At other times, I'd suddenly get an inspiration to take one or more actions, I'd take them, and amazing creations would follow. Life got more and more fun for me—and easier and easier from an energy and effort perspective. All the concepts I've shared with you so far became more and more real to me and my "getting" of them deepened in ways I would have never imagined. Shortly thereafter, I hit the Busting Loose Point, which I'll describe in detail in the next chapter.

| KEY POINT | Busting loose from The Money Game isn't about creating the illusion of more money appearing to flow to you through traditional channels like a business, job, investments, or inheritance, although you can certainly create and play with such illusions if you choose. It's about opening to *Infinite* Abundance and creative opportunity. Infinite is infinite. It's not something you measure, track, or count, as you'll see in the next chapter. |

Please remember that what I just described is only what I created to support myself in busting loose. It was created in response to the limiting patterns and eggs I installed in The Field for myself in Phase 1. It's not a rule or formula for what's required to bust loose. It doesn't mean that's what you'll choose to create for yourself. It doesn't mean you should expect total "disaster" to come down on you, although you might choose to support yourself in busting loose by doing that. You'll create whatever experience supports you best as a unique Infinite Being playing a unique Human Game.

Also remember that I created *severe pain* in my life for a year and a half to ultimately bust loose from The Money Game *forever*. If you choose to create the illusion of a similar level of *intensity and pain*, or perhaps the illusion of even more *intensity and pain*, for a year, two years, even five or ten years, would it be worth it if you could permanently and completely open to your natural state of Infinite Abundance?

You better believe it!

How many people do you know (or have you read about) who start saving, investing, and planning for retirement or to create financial independence in their twenties? Maybe you did that yourself. The average person continues that trend and works very hard, often doing things he or she doesn't enjoy, until they're 65—40-plus years—and in most cases, after all that work and all those years, he or she does *not* achieve the goal of financial independence or a comfortable retirement. To me, no matter how many weeks, months, or years it takes to bust loose, it's worth it, and unlike Phase 1 and The Money Game, if you do the Phase 2 work, you *will* bust loose and you *will* open to the Infinite Abundance that's your natural state.

My client, Pravin Kapadia, from the United Kingdom, created a very different experience when he entered Phase 2 after attending a Busting Loose from The Money Game live event. He first created sales and profits appearing to soar for his business. Then, as a result of creating the illusion of starting a new division of his business, he created the illusion of expenses for launching the new division causing serious cash flow issues for his core business. His core business was still healthy and chugging along (unlike what happened to my business), but he created a temporarily stressful situation to support him in doing the Phase 2 work. He wrote this to me in an e-mail:

> I realized it was my Expanded Self giving me an opportunity to reclaim power from my discomfort with my money situation. I've been using The Process to reclaim power from my *financial crisis* over a period now and amazing changes are taking place, slowly but surely. There's still more reclaiming of power over my financial discomfort to do, but the main thing is I've put full trust in my Expanded Self, and He is clearly managing my financial situation beautifully to support me in doing the Phase 2 work.

Here is Lorie McCloud's story in her own words:

> I'm totally blind but I don't see that as the real problem. Nothing in my life seeming to work anywhere was the real problem, especially abysmal finances. When I was a teenager and young adult, I earnestly wanted to commit suicide. When I discovered there was a way to bust loose from The Money Game, I couldn't sign up fast enough even though I was already in debt and had to put it on my credit card.
>
> After seriously doing the Phase 2 work for just a month, I started to see changes. For one thing, it's nice to know what to do with the negative thoughts and feelings I experience. I get a huge

charge (pun intended) out of diving into them and then divesting them of every bit of power.

The first thing that happened is I tried one of those home Internet businesses. I crashed and burned and lost even more money (that I didn't have to lose) and had to apply The Process to all the shame and feeling of inadequacy that came up. Then I got a letter out of the blue from the social security office saying my monthly payments were going up. They didn't go up a lot, but just the idea that they could increase at all (which supposedly never happens in my situation) meant all barriers to abundance were being removed.

| **KEY POINT** | *Nothing* in the hologram is real, including government institu- |

tions like the Social Security Administration. It's all a creation of Consciousness and can therefore be molded according to the intentions of your Expanded Self.

Mike Roan, a Phase 2 Coaching Program client living in Tokyo, shared this Phase 2 story with me:

When I came back to Japan from my holiday, I took a night flight and arrived very early in the morning. I took the train to Tokyo, which soon became filled with commuters going to work. I was extremely tired, having had an uncomfortable flight with no sleep, and I couldn't avoid falling asleep on the train. When my stop arrived I hauled my suitcase through the crowd and got off, still half asleep. As the train pulled away I realized to my horror I'd left my hand luggage that contained my passport as well as other important and valuable items on the overhead rack in the train. I immediately reported the loss to the railway people and they said they'd do their best to track it down.

I was in such a state of anxiety I could hardly sit down. Grad-ually, it dawned on me that, as an alien living in a foreign country, I had huge, *huge* amounts of power invested in documentation such as my passport and work visas. Indeed, my whole security and way of life appeared to depend on having those documents in my possession and in order!

I went home and was still extremely anxious. Then the train company called and said they'd searched the train and my bag was nowhere to be found. I realized then my only option was to reclaim power from these items and their importance in my life. I spent the next few hours doing that, not trying to get the documents back, just to reclaim the power from my beliefs and the discomfort. Interestingly enough, later that afternoon I got another call from the railway company saying they'd found my bags fully intact and with all the items still inside and would I please come and collect them! What a gift to have that opportunity to reclaim power!

KEY POINT — **When a creation gets popped into your hologram to support you in doing the Phase 2 work, it only stays long enough to support you in doing the work. Once you do the work and the job has been done, the creation will disappear since there's no longer a reason for it to be there.**

My wife Cecily chose to launch herself into Phase 2 with an amazing and incredibly intense experience. Let me first set the stage for the story. Cecily and I have two children, a daughter Ali who is seven, and a son Aidan who is four. At the time, we had two dogs, Mollie and Peri. Our daughter's school had a guinea pig named Cocoa Puff that students could take home to care for and she'd been at our home for two weeks. We were always careful to put the dogs in another room with the door closed whenever we let Cocoa Puff out to play. We also had a young woman we'll call Sally who was a family helper for us, wearing the hat of nanny and personal assistant simultaneously. Finally, on the evening when Cecily launched herself into Phase 2, I was in the middle of conducting a four-day live event. We were on day two and on that second evening, the attendees always came to our home for dinner and socializing. Sally was responsible for setting up the food and drinks and taking care of Ali and Aidan once the party started.

On the afternoon of that day, Cecily was at the event participating as an attendee when she got a call on her cell phone. It was a frantic call from Sally telling Cecily she needed to come home because our dog Mollie had gotten loose and attacked and killed Cocoa Puff. As you might imagine, that made Cecily very uncomfortable. "Oh no," she thought, "we have everyone coming over and there's a dead guinea pig in the house!" Then the thoughts and feelings continued to swirl, "I'm going to have to call the school and tell them we killed their guinea pig. All the kindergarteners who know and love Cocoa Puff will be heartbroken. Ahhhhhh!"

But the creation didn't stop there. Before we allowed Cocoa Puff to come into our home, we'd talked to our daughter Ali about how having a pet is a big responsibility that must be taken seriously. Cecily then created Ali beating herself up with guilt. "I'll never be able to have a pet. I'm not responsible enough, I'm not responsible enough . . ." Ali kept telling herself through the tears.

But the creation didn't stop there. An hour later, all the event attendees arrived at our home and the party started. As the night unfolded, Cecily heard funny noises from upstairs where the kids and Sally were. She ignored them for a while, but they continued so she ultimately went upstairs to check on it. As she walked into Ali's upstairs bathroom, she saw Sally passed out on the floor and Aidan standing naked in the bath with cold water running out of the spout calling "Sally, Sally," trying to wake her up. That was the funny noise Cecily had been hearing. As it turns out, Sally helped herself to some of the wine we had for the party, drank too much, and had passed out from the excess alcohol—*while on duty*. At the time, I didn't know about any of this. Cecily didn't tell me because she didn't want to put a damper on the excitement of the event and the attendees being at our home. Sally had been with us for four months and this was very unusual behavior for her, to say the least.

As Cecily looked at Sally moaning while passed out on the floor and at shivering Aidan calling to her from the bathtub, a gigantic egg that had been partially opened when Cocoa Puff died opened fully for her. "Oh my God," she thought, "I've been trusting my kids to this woman! Bob and I were in London for a week and she was home alone with our kids. Our kids are not safe! Oh ... my ... God! They could have been hurt or killed while we were away! Sally is supposed to come tomorrow when I'm at the event again. What if something happens to the kids while I'm there? She killed a guinea pig and left Aidan alone in the bath and ..."

Cecily began applying The Process and continued applying it for three weeks as the power continued to flow out of that one gigantic egg about the kids being at risk. This whole illusion (and I remind you to look at it as an illusion being played out in a hologram by highly skilled actors) was a brilliant and magnificent creation to give Cecily the opportunity to reclaim massive amounts of power from "power outside" eggs that had been plaguing her all her life. As it turned out, we decided to let Sally go, Cecily did not attend the rest of the live event and applied The Process to all the feelings that surfaced as her creation unfolded and in the months that followed.

KEY POINT	People in your hologram are actors saying and doing what

you ask them to say and do. There's no such thing as in character or out of character. There's just what you ask them to say and do.

Brigitta Neuberger from Vienna was attending a Busting Loose from The Money Game live event from Vienna, Austria. She flew in for the event and had plans to travel throughout the United States after the event before returning home. On the evening of the first day of the event, she created the illusion of misplacing her wallet with all her cash, credit cards, airline tickets, and passport. As she shared this *tragedy* with the group, she was clearly in a state of panic. "Without that wallet, I'm in deep trouble. I can't continue my trip after the event. I have no money for food during the event. I can't even get back home. I looked everywhere. In my hotel room, the event room, my car, all the stores, and restaurants I'd been in. Nothing."

I knew she'd created the illusion of losing her wallet to give herself a great Phase 2 gift. "Brilliant creation," I told her. "You created that to give yourself a great gift. Tomorrow you'll discover a tool I call The Process. Use it. Then just watch. Your wallet will turn up again in some strange way. It's not really gone. You just created the illusion of it being gone to support you in reclaiming power." Sure enough, two days later she came into the session with a huge smile on her face and told the group that she'd been driving her car that morning, jammed on her brakes when the car in front of her stopped suddenly, and lo and behold, she saw her wallet slide out from under the front passenger seat into plain view. "I know I looked under that seat more than once," she assured the group.

Shifting gears, here are some examples of the "expect weird things to happen" aspect of Phase 2 and also how creations can get popped into your hologram to show how powerful you really are and the degree to which you really do create everything you experience, down to the smallest detail. In the Introduction, I mentioned that some of what I'd be sharing with you in this book would sound like science fiction to you. Remember that warning and everything you've learned so far as you dive into the stories that follow.

Dan Cabrera, a client from Illinois, wrote this to me after returning home from a Busting Loose from The Money Game live event:

> My bus ride was truly miraculous. I kept getting proof from my Expanded Self all the way home, from roadside signs, to the remarkable conversations with other travelers that had to do with

busting loose. When I got home, my Expanded Self immediately sent me two creations that caused a lot of discomfort:

1. My daughter was very depressed after losing her three best friends following a disagreement.
2. My sister-in-law in San Diego experienced a major financial fiasco.

Well, remembering what you said, I was moved to say, "Bring it on!!" I began to apply The Process. When I got to my office the next morning and checked e-mail messages, I really felt I was being supported beautifully. Here is an excerpt from the e-mail I received from the chairperson of a department on campus:

> Dan,
>
> We have a need to develop online courses to use in our new undergraduate program to have ready for the Fall 2006 offering. We need to have the following courses developed for online delivery. Additionally, we are look-ing for faculty members who are interested in teaching these courses on-load or off-load. It may be that the online developers and teachers are the same or different persons.
>
> I have listed all the courses below, but think you are a good match for UHHS 410, which is similar to the AHPH course that you have taught before. The college would pay a $3,500 stipend for developing the course. A group of faculty members from the college developed the course outline last summer, so there is a starting place.
>
> We are hoping to offer the class in Fall 2006 or Spring 2007. You could start as soon as you are available. Are you interested in developing this course? Are you interested in teaching this course or others on this list?

In the worksheet I completed before beginning the Busting Loose event, I had expressed a desire to return to being an educator and devoting my time to developing online innovative educational programs to large populations. In your own words, "WOW," and this is just the beginning.

Mike Roan also shared this Phase 2 experience:

While on holiday recently I stayed at my sister's place, and she had a whole series of DVDs by the English naturalist David Attenborough called *The Living Planet*. As I watched the DVDs I really felt in awe of the magnificence and variety of life in the hologram and from a Phase 2 perspective, the incredible creation of this earth and amazement at how I could have created it with such amazing detail, with so many creatures and phenomena and such beauty.

Deborah Mandas, a dentist client of mine, while attending a Busting Loose from The Money Game live event, created a fascinating Phase 2 experience for herself while going out for dinner with other members of the group. Prior to attending the dinner, she looked in her wallet and noticed $300 in it. However, when she opened her wallet again to *pay* for her share of the group dinner, she noticed there was an extra $500 in it. "I'm absolutely certain it was *not* there before and that I didn't miscount," she said.

Michael Hackett, another attendee of a Busting Loose from The Money Game live event, created the following experience to show himself how powerful he was and the fact that he's creating absolutely everything he experiences:

Six of us went out to dinner last night. Because of my financial situation and a few other reasons, I live with my Dad who is 70 years old. We're really close. I just adore him. I called him while we were at dinner to say, "Happy Father's Day," and he said, "You'll never guess what I bought."

"What," I asked.

"A Corvette," he says.

"What do you mean, you bought a Corvette?"

"That's not the good part," he said, "Guess how much it cost me."

"What?"

"$100."

It turns out he bought a raffle ticket three months prior from a public broadcasting station and they'd just called to tell him he'd won a 2005 Corvette. My dad has had injuries to his knee. He's about 6'2″ and has a hard time bending that leg. You can't get him into an ordinary car, so he drives a minivan instead. I was just so excited for him, just so happy. So I said, "What are you going to do with the Corvette?"

"Oh, I'm just going to take the money."

"How much is that?"

"Oh, it's at least $40,000. Maybe more," he said.

It doesn't matter to me if I ever see a dollar of that money or not. The whole thing just popped in out of left field. Looking at this from a Phase 2 perspective, I realized there was no raffle, no raffle ticket, and no three-month time lag in which my father was supposedly holding the ticket. All of a sudden I said to myself, "Michael, you created the entire thing! You just—poof—created the whole thing, including the story that he got the raffle ticket." I really got how powerful I am and how amazing this whole game is. That was exciting.

One of the other attendees of the event who was at dinner with Michael when he found out about the Corvette added this:

I was there to experience it, and it was amazing because we all felt there was a great message for all of us in the story. Then another thing happened. Michael's been very honest with us about his financial situation. In fact, he's quite short of cash at the moment. After he ended his phone call with his dad, all of a sudden, out of the blue, as another round of beers was being delivered to the table, the waiter came up, handed *Michael* another beer and said, "That's free because it's the last of the tap."

So we're all looking at Michael after the Corvette story, and then he gets this free beer. And we're thinking, "Whoa! He's got the touch." About 15 minutes after that, the waiter came back and announced they had found some more beer, and Michael could have another beer if he wanted—but he'd have to pay for it.

When this story was related to me and the group during a live session, I said the following:

> Get the significance of this beyond the laughing. There's no restaurant. There's no waiter. There's no beer. Michael created the illusion of the beer being the last in the tap. Michael created the illusion of the waiter giving him a free beer, supposedly for that reason. When's the last time you saw a restaurant give you something for free because it's the last one they have? It makes no sense. But the waiter was just an actor saying and doing what Michael asked him to so it didn't need to make sense. It just needed to support Michael in doing the Phase 2 work, which it did.
>
> It's interesting that Michael is starting with little stuff. As time passes and he reclaims more power, the kinds of things he creates for himself will expand, as he opens into *knowing* more and more is possible for him. Once you have enough experiences of how powerful you really are, and you will, you can't deny that what I've been sharing with you is true.

As another example, I have a client named Jeff Priestley from the United Kingdom who sent me the following story:

> It was Sunday morning and I was watching a TV program (*Gilmore Girls*), a favorite show of mine. It began at 10:00 A.M. I'd watched the first 10 minutes of the show when my wife called out to say she'd run a bath for me. I went upstairs and had a leisurely bath followed by a shave followed by getting dressed. Doing all that normally takes me 30 minutes or more. However, when I came downstairs again, it was only 10:15 A.M. on that same clock. I was astounded and checked the other clocks in the house and they all showed the same time. My TV program was still on and still at the 15 minutes into it part of the show. Amazed, I watched the show for another 45 minutes until it finished. I guess time is one of the ultimate limitations and illusions that until now I'd taken for granted. Obviously, my Expanded Self thought otherwise.

Cecily created another amazing experience to show herself how powerful she is. She was on a long driving trip with our daughter Ali. They were tired and decided to stop for the night, so Cecily started looking for signs for an exit off the highway that had a hotel available. She soon saw a sign and drove onto the exit ramp. At the bottom of the ramp was a sign showing that a Hampton Inn was one-third of a mile to the right. Cecily turned right and went one-third of a mile. No hotel. Half a mile. No hotel. Two miles. No hotel.

She backtracked two miles, stopped at a gas station and asked about the hotel. "Yep, third of a mile on the right. You can't miss it. Big blue and red sign," the clerk told her. So, she turned right out of the gas station and drove the third of a mile, then half a mile, then two miles again. No hotel! At first she was frustrated but reclaimed power from it and ultimately remembered she was in Phase 2 and started to laugh. She got back on the highway and drove for a while until she saw another exit with a hotel off it. She followed the directions again. No hotel! This repeated four more times before a hotel was finally where it was *supposed* to be.

So, I ask you, is *anything* in the hologram real, solid, or stable? No!

I created a similar illusion when I was driving home from a business trip to Washington, DC. I asked the hotel concierge for directions back to the highway I needed to drive on to get home. The directions were very simple. I followed the first few directions. No problem. Then the directions said, "Drive for 8 miles until you see exit 9 and get off at exit 9." I was driving along and saw exit 7, exit 8, then exit 10. No exit 9! I drove on for a while, got off at exit 13 and looped around, going back the opposite way on the same highway. I then saw exit 12, exit 11, exit 10, then . . . exit 8. No exit 9! Since I created a pattern of always getting lost in Phase 1, I started to get frustrated and applied The Process.

I then got lost trying to loop around again and ended up driving into Ronald Reagan airport which made me angry again. I applied

The Process. When I finally figured out how to get out of the airport and back onto the highway, the same thing happened again—exit 7, exit 8, exit 10. No exit 9! I had now un-created exit 9 three times. It repeated another two times before I finally saw exit 9 and was able to get off and drive home. Now, you can say to yourself, "You just spaced out. Exit 9 was there all along and you just missed it." Number one, I'm not that spacey, but even if I was capable of missing it once, I'm not capable of missing it five times, especially when I was on hyper alert after missing it the first few times.

So, I ask you, is *anything* in the hologram real, solid, or stable? No!

Ronald Saven, another coaching client of mine, called and told me of an amazing creation he popped into his hologram. He told me how he'd arranged for a transfer of $50,000 from one of his accounts to another. The second account had $1,000 in it. When he looked at the balance in the second account the next day, instead of having $51,000 in it, it had $101,000 in it! He created $50,000 out of thin air—which is all money and numbers really are anyway! In Truth, there was no bank, no $50,000, no funds transfer, and no $101,000. It was all made up. All an illusion. All a magnificent creation designed by Ronald to show himself how powerful he really is and how morphable the hologram really is—by Consciousness.

Now, from a Phase 1 perspective, it would be easy to say, "That's no big deal and it's perfectly understandable. The bank simply made an error in the transfer. It will discover it and take the extra money back." You could choose to interpret it that way. However, Ronald and I chose to interpret it from a Phase 2 perspective from which it's perfectly explainable, too. A pattern was created in The Field for the $50,000, the transfer, and the $101,000 in the second account. Power was added to it, and the illusion of an account with $101,000 popped into Ronald's hologram appearing to be real. By the way, at the time of this writing, the extra $50,000 is still in his imaginary account.

So, I ask you again, is *anything* in the hologram real, solid, or stable?

No!

Earlier in this chapter I shared how I'd created $210,000 in two minutes. Let me now share the details of that story. It began early in my Phase 2 experience when my friend Randy Gage invited me to speak at a convention for the National Speakers Association (NSA) in Cancun, Mexico. I was invited to speak about a marketing model I'd developed for selling high-ticket items from Internet web sites. I didn't receive any *fee* for the talk, although my *expenses* were paid by NSA. Randy told me, "Normally you can't do it at NSA events, but at this one, if you want to sell products or services from the stage and make some money, you can do it."

I knew my marketing model could work magic for the professional speakers who were attending the convention, and I was excited about sharing the details with them. I didn't go to make any money, however. There's nothing wrong with making money, that just wasn't my motivation at the time because I was deeply immersed in doing the Phase 2 work. When I got on the plane, I had no intention of selling anything from the stage, just sharing what I had to share, having fun doing the talk and where it led it led. However, when I got there, I started thinking, "You know something, it might be fun to coach a few people on applying the model because I love working with it." So, I typed up a quick document outlining what I'd offer through a one-year coaching program and what the expression of appreciation (which I still called investment at the time) would be for working with me. The number I felt inspired to *charge* for the program was $17,500. I'd never offered a coaching program like that before. I just felt motivated to do it. I didn't care if no one signed up or a hundred people signed up. I just felt motivated to do it. Remember, that's how you live in Phase 2.

I spoke for three hours. I gave it my all and shared everything I knew. Then, at the end of the talk, I still felt motivated to offer the coaching program so I simply said this: "If any of you would like my help over the next year to execute what you've just discovered, I have a coaching program available and there are applications up here." I got mobbed! People were grabbing at the applications like they were $1,000 bills. More people applied than I could possibly accept, but I accepted 12 people I felt I could have a lot of fun helping. The appreciation expressed (in the form of money) by the 12 people enrolling into the program amounted to an instant illusory $210,000.

Let me share another fascinating example of how it can look to play The Human Game in Phase 2. When I first started playing the direct response marketing and mail-order games, as part of locking myself into The Money Game and limitation in Phase 1, I created the illusion of what's called a money-back guarantee. When playing those games, you want to sell as much product as you possibly can. Since the belief is that other people have their own power and independent decision-making authority, you must therefore be extremely persuasive to get them to buy your products. It then follows that if you could reverse the risk to a buyer by offering their money back if they're not 100 percent satisfied, more people would buy. Makes sense, right? Absolutely. I bought into it hook, line, and sinker for 18 years.

I even used the creation of a money-back guarantee to contribute to my Phase 1 crash and burn experience. At the time, I'd been running a mail-order business for two years. It was very successful and all the numbers were very predictable. I'd get so many leads per month, a certain percentage would buy, and a certain percentage would send the product back for a refund. Suddenly, however, I created sales dropping through the floor and refunds skyrocketing and that trend continued for a year, which ultimately caused the business to fail and me to *lose* a lot of money. As a result, I created an intense dislike for refunds that lasted for many years.

As I moved into Phase 2 many years later and was running other businesses that sold products through the mail, ads in magazines, and over the Internet, I still offered a money-back guarantee, people still took me up on it, and I still gave people refunds if they weren't satisfied. However, I continued having an intense dislike for refunds and got angry whenever we had to process one.

After applying The Process to my discomfort about refunds for several months, I woke up one morning and thought, "Wait a minute!

There's no one out there. There's no one I need to persuade about anything. They're all just actors saying and doing what I ask them to say and do. It's not possible for them to be dissatisfied with anything I create. All I can do is create the illusion of people being dissatisfied and asking for refunds and convince myself it's real." That morning I removed money-back guarantees from all my business activities.

As you might imagine, after 18 years of belief in the need for guarantees, I had a lot of discomfort about the decision and fear that sales might drop as a result. I therefore applied The Process to the discomfort whenever it came up. At first, as a sign of how patterns in The Field were changing, I created a few people calling or e-mailing us asking if we had a money-back guarantee and if so, what the terms were. I interpreted those creations to mean that I still had some power in the money-back guarantee egg and I continued applying the treasure hunting tools to the creation called refunds. After another few months, all the power in guarantees and refunds had been drained out of the egg and they no longer have any presence in my hologram.

| **KEY POINT** | Once you cross the Busting Loose Point, absolutely everything in your hologram has a question mark after it and absolutely nothing is etched in stone.

Let me share two final brief stories with you. As part of my Phase 2 experience, I created the illusion of gaining 25 pounds in extra weight on my body. As a result, I also created the illusion of most of my pants no longer fitting. I used to wear waist size 33, but had to go out and buy waist size 36 to be comfortable. I bought three pairs of new blue jeans, size 36, from the same manufacturer. I tried them on in the dressing room. All three pairs felt the same on me. Same pants. Same size. Same style. Yet, when I got home, I created the illusion of one pair fitting perfectly, one feeling too tight, and one being so loose it almost fell off. I also created one of my old pairs of jeans, size 33, fitting perfectly.

.ything in the hologram real, solid, or stable?

No!

One of my passions is video production work. I loved creating multimedia presentations to invite people into my sphere of influence and also to deliver what I call remote learning tools. I use a software program to convert those presentations into a specific format called Flash so I can stream them on the Internet. One afternoon, I'd just finished three videos and was using the software to convert the files. When the conversion finished and the video started playing, it was upside down! I called the tech support department for the software company, asked them about it, and was told "That's impossible. There's no possible way the software could do that."

I ask you one final time, is anything in the hologram real, solid, or stable?

No!

Hear me now. Nothing in your hologram is real. It's all made up. It's all a creation of your Consciousness. Exits off the highway can be uncreated by changing one small detail in a pattern in The Field. $101,000 can be created in a bank account by changing one small detail in a pattern in The Field. Twelve people can be created to express $17,500 in appreciation for a coaching program by changing one small detail in a pattern in The Field. Blue jeans can appear to shrink and expand by changing one small detail in a pattern in The Field. A video can appear to be upside down by changing one small detail in a pattern in The Field—even if it's labeled impossible from a Phase 1 perspective.

As I explained, I could go on and on with the stories, and if you make the commitment to the Phase 2 work, you'll create many of your own. Here's the key point to get: If reality is so unstable, so unsolid, and can be so easily molded by a simple shift in Consciousness and a pattern in The Field, what might be possible for you when you bust loose and can play The Human Game without limits or restrictions of any kind? What amazing creations could you pop into your hologram to play with and have an absolute blast as you do? Turn the page and continue on to Chapter 13 to find out.

13

Playing without Limits or Restrictions

Do not follow where the path may lead. Go instead where there is no path and leave a trail.[1]

—Muriel Strode

There are no rules of architecture for a castle in the clouds.[2]

—G. K. Chesterton, Writer (1874–1936)

It's kind of fun to do the impossible.[3]

—Walt Disney

Note: Did you jump forward to this chapter without reading all of the preceding chapters? If so, for your sake, please go back and finish the others before reading this. You won't be able to bust loose unless you receive all the puzzle pieces I have for you, the whole busting loose map pops into view, and you can then use that map to actually bust loose. Trust me on this!

In the last few chapters, I explained that living in Phase 2 means applying the four treasure hunting tools day after day without an agenda, an investment in results or specific outcomes, or a desire to fix, change, or improve your hologram. I explained that in Phase 2, you live in reactive mode, taking life a moment at a time, waiting to see what gets popped into your hologram, then responding as you feel motivated or inspired to—before or after applying The Process to reclaim power from discomfort that arises.

When you do that enough, and I can't tell you what enough means for you because we're all different, you reach the Busting Loose Point, then cross it into a new world and a new way of living. You're now ready to discover what the Busting Loose Point is all about and to see what it looks like once you cross it. Keep in mind, however, that while your Busting Loose Point will have several things in common with mine and that of *other people*, you'll ultimately customize your Busting Loose Point and what follows to support yourself as a unique Infinite Being playing a unique Human Game.

| KEY POINT | **Every Infinite Being creates His or Her own unique Busting** |

Loose Point and what comes before and after crossing it. See Figure 13.1 for a visual you can use to internalize what it looks and feels like to cross the Busting Loose Point.

Also keep in mind that what I'm sharing in this chapter isn't theory or a narrative of something I simply *believe* is possible. I reached the Busting Loose Point, crossed it, and I'm actually living in the ways I discuss in this chapter. My journey is far from over, however. I'm still using the treasure hunting tools on a daily basis, expanding at an ever-accelerating pace and expressing more and more of who I really am in my hologram. I don't know how deep the rabbit hole actually goes in Phase 2, nor do I want to know. I prefer to allow the magnificence of Phase 2 to unfold on its own and to surprise and delight me. I must say that even though I have no idea of what it will look like as I move more deeply into Phase 2, going as deeply into it as I have at the time of this writing has been more

FIGURE 13.1   The Busting Loose Point.

incredible than anything I've ever experienced or ever thought I would experience.

When you cross the Busting Loose Point, you've collapsed the foundational patterns that kept you locked into financial limitation, and you've expanded and opened to the Infinite Abundance that's your natural state. At that moment, you *know*—at a very deep and profound level—you're creating absolutely everything you experience. You *know*—from deep within your Being—you have the power to create absolutely anything and pop it into your hologram to play with. You *know*—from deep within your Being—that numbers aren't real, money isn't real, your accounts aren't real, the apparent flow of money through your hologram isn't real, and your natural state of Infinite Abundance *is* real. You have total trust and confidence in The Truth of who you really are. This is a very real and very attainable state of Consciousness, even if it seems like science fiction right now.

As a result, once you cross the Busting Loose Point, there's no longer a *need* to check your bank balances, or financial statements, and if you still do, you look at the numbers with amusement and appreciation while knowing The Truth about them. There's no longer any *need* to track or measure the apparent flow of money. *Cost* is irrelevant. *Bills* have no significance.

> **KEY POINT** After crossing the Busting Loose Point, you just express appreciation for all the creations you choose to experience (in the illusory form of cash, checks, credit cards, or other transfers) with absolute certainty that your Infinite Abundance is real and the money will take care of itself—however it takes care of itself.

Then money *does* take care of itself—however it takes care of itself. You have no limits or restrictions of any kind as it relates to money. In Phase 1, you convinced yourself if you want to buy or do something, you must have the money first and then you can buy or do it. In Phase 1, if you have the money, great. If you don't, you've got to save up until you have enough to buy or do what you want, or borrow the money and then pay it back with interest. After you cross the Busting Loose Point, that dynamic reverses itself. You feel motivated or inspired to express appreciation for specific creations *first*, you express the appreciation, and the money takes care of itself—however it takes care of itself. I keep saying "however it takes care of itself" because as you'll see, there's no fixed or set way for that to happen after you cross the Busting Loose Point. Why? Because infinite is infinite and no limits really means no limits! I'll give you several examples of how it *can* look later in the chapter, but those are just examples, not rules, formulas, or limits.

| KEY POINT | After you cross the Busting Loose Point, money *can* still |

appear to come from the hologram (although it doesn't need to) but you'll *know* it doesn't. You'll *know* it comes from you, your Consciousness, a pattern in The Field, and your power. The story line of how it appears to show up is just how you chose to express your Infinite Abundance for maximum enjoyment and fun.

Expressing appreciation in the form of money then becomes like breathing. You don't worry about where your next breath will come from, do you? You don't measure or track how much air is available to you right now—or how much will be available to you in the future. You don't try to get more air or protect the air you already have. You just breathe without thinking about it, and you have total faith that the air will always be there for you. Living from your natural state of Infinite Abundance works the same way. You just breathe your abundance.

Here's another way to look at what opening to your Infinite Abundance looks and feels like after you cross the Busting Loose Point. I call it *Cosmic Overdraft Protection*. In banking, there's a Phase 1 creation called overdraft protection. In case you're not familiar with it, here's how it works. Your checking account is linked to a credit card or other account. If you write a check and there isn't enough money in your checking account to cover it, the funds automatically get transferred from your credit card or the other account and the check is made good.

Imagine what life would be like for you and how it would change if you had overdraft protection where the other account was your natural state of Infinite Abundance which had an unlimited supply of money in it. Imagine what your life would be like and how it would change if you had absolute confidence in your Cosmic Overdraft Protection and you could just follow what brings you joy, fully immerse yourself in creative ecstasy, do what you want to do, appreciate your creations, write checks as expressions of that appreciation, and know that all those checks would be *made good*, too.

| KEY POINT | You qualify for Cosmic Overdraft Protection the minute you cross the Busting Loose Point. |

You qualify for Cosmic Overdraft Protection the minute you cross the Busting Loose Point.

When I first reached the Busting Loose Point, saw what was beyond it, and knew—intellectually—that everything I just shared was the absolute Truth, I still couldn't live and breathe it. The thought of blindly expressing appreciation and writing checks without tracking the numbers, just trusting that the money would take care of itself, scared me every time I entertained actually doing it.

Despite how far I'd come, how much power I'd reclaimed, and how much I'd expanded, I still had power in eggs that caused me to fear getting bounced check notices from my bank, getting angry phone calls from vendors, my credit rating going to hell, and so on—and those fears kept me from crossing the Busting Loose Point. In other words, I was in a sort of no man's land.

Then, one day, after applying The Process extensively to those fears, I had a revelation when my Expanded Self said this to me in a meditation: "As long as you understand about breathing your abundance but don't actually start breathing, you're saying 'My Infinite Abundance isn't really there,' or 'It may not really be there'—and you continue to feed power into your financial limitation eggs. At some point, you've got to make a decision about what's real and what's not, draw a line in the sand, cross it, and never go back. You can't stay in no man's land and fully open to your Infinite Abundance."

I *knew* those words were True and I so badly wanted to bust loose from The Money Game, but it still felt unsafe, like jumping off a cliff without a net. I continued applying The Process to my fears until one day I woke up and said, "I'm jumping off the cliff today. I have no choice but to trust that my Expanded Self is going to support me perfectly as I 'fall.'" On that day, I started acting as if my

Infinite Abundance was real, as if I really had Cosmic Overdraft Protection, as if every time I put a dollar into the slot machine, I'd get three dollars back. I stopped watching the numbers. I stopped logging onto my online banking resources. I stopped studying my financial statements.

Once I made that decision, I created numerous opportunities to express appreciation in the form of money. Sometimes I expressed it in a joyful and expanded state. At other times (a lot at first but then less and less), when I first saw the *bill*, or signed a check, fear still came up in varying intensities, so I applied The Process. Through it all, I kept breathing. I kept acting as if The Truth was The Truth— and my Infinite Abundance was real. That's what I did for another six months until I finally crossed the Busting Loose Point, and was never short of financial "air" again!

By the way, what I just described is *not* the same thing as the popular phrase "fake it till you make it." That concept is a Phase 1 creation that does not and cannot work in Phase 2. In fact, it never really works in Phase 1 either, although many people swear by it. The reason I was able to make the transition I just described is because I'd reclaimed so much power, expanded so much, and most importantly, was being fully supported in making the leap by my Expanded Self.

Once you cross the Busting Loose Point, your natural state of Infinite Abundance expresses itself however you choose to express it. As I mentioned in the last few chapters, infinite means infinite. It means no limits whatsoever. Money can *appear* to move through your hologram, but it doesn't need to any longer. It can simply show up in your checking account without any apparent source—like the story I shared in the last chapter about the extra $50,000 that ended up in my client's account.

If you do create money appearing to move through your hologram from an apparent source, you could pop it into your hologram by finding a briefcase filled with cash on the street (a personal fantasy of mine I've not yet created but may one day). Your Infinite Abundance might express itself as the illusion of *other people* expressing appreciation for you in the form of money. For example,

I have a friend who's playing the Phase 2 game. He wrote a book 20 years ago. One of his readers who read the book and used what he learned to create tremendous success for himself (in the illusion, of course), sent my friend a large check with a note saying, "I read your book and it really helped me. This is just a small token of my appreciation for what you did for me. Keep up the great work."

If you look at my life as an example, since I've created the illusion of owning businesses that offer products and services, I could choose to express my Infinite Abundance by asking actors to play the role of customers expressing appreciation for those products and services in whatever quantity I choose. I could also choose to express appreciation for myself in the form of money by selling one of the businesses and creating the illusion of receiving a large check. As I explained in the Introduction, I actually created that illusion when we sold Blue Ocean Software for $177 million in cash.

You could express your Infinite Abundance through an unexpected inheritance. As I say that, you might think to yourself, "I don't know anyone who could leave me an inheritance of any significance." If you had a thought like that, remember that everything you experience is a creation of your Consciousness from a pattern you inserted into The Field, and you can insert *any* pattern into The Field. It doesn't have to make sense or be logical which are just limited Phase 1 creations. Once you pass the Busting Loose Point, you can create *anything* you want to play with just for the sheer pleasure of playing with it.

Let me give you an extreme example to illustrate the power and true meaning of what I just shared. At the time of this writing, Bill Gates is the world's richest man. If you wanted to, if it would really support you on your journey, *in your hologram*, you could create Bill Gates dying and leaving you $10 million in his will. Now, you might say "Why on earth would Bill Gates do that? I don't even know him." The odds are slim you'd choose to create that illusion in your hologram, but the point is, *you could*. You have the power and ability to do it. Why? Because it's just another pattern in The Field and Bill Gates is just another actor who would do what you asked him to do—*in your hologram*—if you really wanted to create that illusion. Remember, in this example, there's no Bill Gates, no dying, no will, no $10 million. You could make up any story you wanted for why Bill Gates would leave you so much money and pop it into your hologram appearing to be real. It's all just details in a pattern in The Field. I realize this is probably tweaking with your head, but you're ready now to be fully open to The Truth, no matter how much it challenges your old belief systems.

| KEY POINT | Infinite is infinite. There are no limits of any kind once you cross the Busting Loose Point. It's just a question of how you want to play The Human Game and what would be fun and joyful for you. |

So, once you cross the Busting Loose Point, does it mean you can go around expressing appreciation in the form of money in the millions to buy mansions, private jets, fancy cars, and *expensive* clothes without giving it a second thought? You could certainly do that if you reclaim enough power, collapse enough limiting patterns in The Field, open enough into your Infinite Abundance—*and, most importantly, if it would really bring you joy.* There's no judgment in Phase 2—no right, wrong, should, should not, good, bad, better, or worse. You can literally create whatever you want. However, it's possible that such creations will no longer interest you after you do the Phase 2 work and continue expanding.

I can tell you that at this point on my Phase 2 journey, those big money attractions in the amusement park hold little interest for me, although they once did. Many desires for things ultimately come from judgments and illusions in the Phase 1 Game that ultimately fall away on their own as you do the Phase 2 work, open up to who you really are, and expand. I've created a beautiful home in a beautiful community in which to live. I drive a luxury car, stay in fine hotels, eat in fine restaurants, and enjoy many luxuries. What's most important to me, however, is the joy and satisfaction I feel from moving more deeply into Phase 2, living in creative ecstasy, and continually expressing more of who I really am in my hologram.

| KEY POINT | Each time you apply The Process, you expand, change, and actually become a different person who desires different things. That's another reason for taking life one moment at a time in Phase 2. Why plan for the future, even just a few days forward, when you don't know who you'll be or what you'll want when you get there (i.e., create it)?

Most of the examples I just gave you involve the illusion of money still appearing to move through the hologram in visible and countable fashion. It may seem like if you created such illusions, you'd still be playing The Money Game and still be focusing on piling up money. However, once you cross the Busting Loose Point, that's not what it's about. For example, at the time of this writing, I still have multiple businesses and money still appears to move through them. However, I don't care about the numbers or how big they appear to be. It's no longer about products, services, customers, sales, profits, income, salary, and so on. It's about me and my fun and enjoyment. I'm just playing in creative ecstasy, expressing massive appreciation for myself, the creations I genuinely want to experience, The Human Game itself—and the rest, including money, takes care of itself.

For example, when I created 12 people expressing appreciation of $17,500 each for my one year coaching program ($210,000), I looked at that number when I created it. It was fun to see such a big number result from a brief mention of the coaching program when I would have worked a lot harder in Phase 1 to generate an equal amount. However, beyond that, the number $210,000 had no significance for me. I didn't need the money to *pay bills* or *improve* my lifestyle. It didn't make anything possible that wasn't already possible for me. The money wasn't real and had no power. Why? Because I was already breathing! The day may come when it no longer interests me to run businesses or see money appearing to move in my hologram. As I said, I'm nowhere near the end of my Phase 2 journey.

> **KEY POINT** The *what* you do in Phase 2 doesn't matter. *How* and *why* you do it and the overall level of joyfulness and fun you receive from the experience is what matters.

The ultimate goal of Phase 2 is to play The Human Game without any limits or restrictions. That really means *no limits or restrictions*. You can create and play with anything, no matter how Phase 1 it may appear from a certain perspective. You can play business games with no limits or restrictions. You can play medical games with no limits or restrictions. You can play war games, parenting games, teaching games, writing games, painting games, or space travel games with no limits or restrictions.

I just watched a documentary about how coral reefs around the world are in danger and may disappear in the next 20 or 30 years if we don't do something. You can play save the reef games or prevent global warming games or get the world to recycle games or create electric cars games as a friend of mine is doing.

You can create the illusion of being an actor, musician, professional athlete, CEO of a multimillion or multibillion dollar corporation, or anchor on the nightly news—just for the sheer pleasure of doing it—even if you don't currently have the skill, track record, connections or, whatever else you imagine would be needed to do it. In Phase 2, you can play *any* game in the amusement park if it floats your boat—or create entirely new games to play that no one has ever thought of before (which is what I personally believe many Infinite Beings will do as they move more deeply into Phase 2).

> **KEY POINT** In Phase 2, you can play any game you want, even if it still appears to be a Phase 1 game. You just play differently. You can also create entirely new games no one has ever thought of before.

When I first created the illusion of releasing the ideas you're discovering here to the public, I created two women buying my *7 Power Centers of Life* home study course. Both women were practitioners of holistic healing or what you might call alternative medicine techniques. After completing the course, they both sent me e-mails expressing ideas like this in a total panic: "My whole career is based around the body being real, illness being real, and my techniques being able to really heal people. If nothing is real, what am I supposed to do, quit?"

I wrote them back and said this: "You can do anything you want in Phase 2. If you really enjoy playing the healing game, you can certainly continue playing. You'll then continue creating people coming to you with all sorts of illnesses and you'll continue creating all kinds of healing techniques to help them—all in support of you playing the healing game with maximum fun and enjoyment. However, if you're doing that work out of obligation, because someone pushed you into it, to make money, or for some other reason, and it really *doesn't* bring you joyfulness or perhaps even bores you, either now, or at some point in the future after you continue expanding, you also have the opportunity to make another choice."

One of the women discovered she really did have a genuine love for the healing game and continued playing it. The other woman ultimately quit and went in a different creative direction as she moved more deeply into Phase 2.

I have several friends who love trading stocks and commodities. I know others who love buying and selling real estate. I know others who love teaching how to buy and sell stocks, commodities, and real estate. Looking at those activities from one perspective, they're pure Phase 1 Money Game activities. However, when played after crossing the Busting Loose Point, they become completely different games and are played in completely different ways. If you chose to play the stocks and commodities game after crossing the Busting Loose Point, for example, you'd create the illusion of up and down movements in the markets, buying, selling, profits, and losses in a way that would be fun for you. It would all be about *your fun*. There would be no limits or restrictions on what's possible for you to create and experience.

If you chose to play the Real Estate Game after busting loose, you'd create the illusion of land, homes, buildings, buyers, sellers, and transfers of property appearing to move in ways that would be fun for you for the sheer pleasure of playing that game—and you might do it in a way no one has ever done or even thought of before. There would be no limits or restrictions on what you did or how you did it.

If you chose to teach others how to play the make money through trading stocks, commodities, and real estate games, you'd create as many people as you wanted to come into your sphere of influence and attend your seminars, hire you to speak, or buy your books, tapes, courses, consulting, and coaching services—and you might do it in a way no one has ever done or even thought of before. There would be no limits or restrictions on what's possible.

The numbers associated with playing all those games—sales, expenses, income, profits, asset value, net worth, and so on—would be irrelevant unless looking at and tracking them *from a Phase 2 perspective* would be fun for you.

As long as you continue playing The Human Game, you'll choose rides or attractions from the amusement park to play with, or create entirely new ones. Therefore, as long as you continue playing The Human Game, you'll still be creating and playing with illusions that come from patterns in The Field. You'll still allow things to appear to unfold over the illusion of time, versus snapping your fingers and making them appear instantly. Why? Because the illusions you create and pop into your hologram will be thrilling for you to experience in exactly that way.

KEY POINT In Phase 2, nothing is about *other people* anymore. It's all about you, your fun, your joy, your expansion, and everyone else comes along for the ride to support you in playing your games.

Let me give you an example to illustrate this key point. Last July, a friend of mine named Lee approached me and asked if I wanted to partner with him in creating a new business to offer a course of study based on his work. I liked Lee very much and was also very excited about his work. My primary focus in the partnership would be in helping him create multimedia promotional materials and course elements. I felt motivated to get involved and accepted his invitation. I was actively playing the Phase 2 game at the time.

Now, in Phase 1, this opportunity would have been about:

- Helping Lee spread the word about his work
- Helping clients benefit from his work
- Making as much money as possible through doing the first two items

In Phase 2, however, *in my hologram* (remember, we don't concern ourselves with what's going on in someone else's hologram), this isn't about Lee, his work, his clients, or making money. It's about me. It's about me supporting myself in doing the Phase 2 work, having fun and playing in Phase 2. I will therefore carve this opportunity by creating Lee and his staff acting in certain ways, prospects and clients acting in certain ways, and creating opportunities to use my multimedia tools and skills for maximum joy, fun, and to deepen my journey into Phase 2. As I mentioned previously, the story line doesn't matter. The details are irrelevant. Everything that happens with this business will come from patterns in The Field I insert there to support me in playing in Phase 2 the way I want to play. Once again you see that everything in Phase 2 is the exact opposite of how it is in Phase 1.

Let me give you another example. You're no doubt familiar with the Harry Potter phenomenon. In that particular illusion, J. K. Rowling wrote the first book out of pure inspiration. She had no desire or intention for the book to become a runaway bestseller, for the other books in the series to become runaway bestsellers, for the books to lead to movies that became box office smashes, or to become one of the world's wealthiest people—virtually overnight—through the experience. She felt compelled to write the book, she wrote it, and released it to the public. It then appeared to take on a life of its own and through a series of magical events (pun intended), become an incredibly wild and exciting no limits ride for her in the amusement park. The first book in the series was published in 1997, so at the time of this writing, that ride has lasted nine years so far.

As I look at that example, being a writer and someone who has always had a passion for the movie industry, I think it would be an absolute blast to take a wild and exciting no limits ride like that—write a series of books, have them take off like a rocket through a series of magical and unintended events, and have the rocket launch open doors to other thrilling experiences, including movies being made from the books. I may choose to create an experience like that in Phase 2. I may not. But if I did, I'd create patterns in The Field that would make it appear to unfold one day at a time—with absolutely no limits on what I could create—through the illusion of time (just as Rowling's experience did), and with various people playing various roles to enhance my enjoyment of the experience—for however long I wanted to extend the ride. I'd savor every second of that unfolding, thrilling at the surprise of what pops into my hologram each day along the way. That's what Phase 2 is all about. I wouldn't just snap my fingers, create the illusion of the final result, then say, "Okay, poof, I just sold 20 million books and racked up two billion in sales from five movies. Great. What's next?" Why? Because there's no fun in that!

| KEY POINT | Opening to your Infinite Abundance means letting go of |

thoughts and concerns about how you will receive it or how you must act to receive it.

When I was playing The Money Game in Phase 1, I immersed myself deeply within creations called the mail-order business and

e marketing. I spent 18 years playing those games and
terful player. Based on what I'm seeing unfold in my
̲̲̲̲̲ ̲ experience, I don't see myself doing any one thing for
a long period of time again. The way my Phase 2 experience is
unfolding, it's more like surfing. I create a particular wave coming in
that looks interesting so I get up on my board and start riding it until
I feel like getting off. Then I get off and wait until another wave I
created starts to roll, jump on when I feel so moved, then ride that
wave for as long as I choose to, then get off again—continuously
creating new kinds of waves to ride as I continue expanding.

I'm sure everything I just described seems very exciting to you.
However, does it still seem hard to believe, like a pie in the sky fantasy? If thoughts like that crossed your mind, it's perfectly understandable for you to feel that way, given the Phase 1 limiting beliefs
you still have huge amounts of power in. However, I assure you, it's
absolutely real, and if you accept my invitation in Chapter 15, leap
into Phase 2 and use your treasure hunting tools in the ways I've
suggested, you *will get there*. As I've mentioned, if you still have
doubts but make the commitment, your Expanded Self will give you
proof of the Truthfulness of all of this through the experiences you
create and pop into your hologram. I absolutely guarantee it.

Let's take a moment to ground what I just shared by returning
to science. I explained earlier that once you pass the Busting Loose
Point, you no longer need to pay attention to numbers or count,
measure or track the flow of money in your life (unless you choose
to do it from a Phase 2 perspective). Let's take another look at that
concept from the perspective of quantum physics. You know that
science looks at The Field as a source of unlimited power and infinite potential. When Consciousness focuses on The Field, a specific creation, a single possibility collapses out of it as determined by
the intention of Consciousness.

Who you really are is pure Consciousness. Who you really are is
Infinite Power and Infinite Abundance, just as science defines The
Field to be. You can't see or experience anything in your hologram
that doesn't originate from a pattern you inserted into The Field.

Therefore, in your hologram, if you decide you w'
balance in your checking account, the balance i.
or other numbers that appear important, what must ha_{r.}
Expanded Self must create a pattern in The Field with spec..
details relating to the account and the numbers you want to see.
Power must then be applied to the pattern, and the details must be
popped into your hologram so there's something for you to see. Oth-
erwise, nothing would be there! The minute your Expanded Self
does that, going back to quantum physics, infinite potential *must*
collapse into a finite, limited creation, right? And whatever you see
must be less than who you really are and what your natural state of
Infinite Abundance really is.

Stick with me here because when you get the significance of this
it'll blow your mind. What would happen, after you pass the Busting
Loose Point, if you simply didn't look at or focus on accounts, statements, or numbers at all? If you don't look, there's no need for a collapse from infinite to finite, right? There's no need to create a
pattern in The Field with details about limited numbers or imaginary
accounts and pop it into your hologram for you to see, is there?
You're just pure Consciousness then, just an Infinite Being playing in
creative ecstasy with infinite potential, right? You're just expressing
appreciation for the creations you choose to experience while living
in a highly expanded state. That's why you don't need to pay attention to the numbers in Phase 2 and why you can simply express
appreciation for your creations with absolute trust and confidence
that the money will take care if itself! You may want to re-read the
last few paragraphs again before you continue. This is where you can
truly go after crossing the Busting Loose Point!

In her book, *Consciousness and Quantum Behavior*, Barbara
Dewey wrote:

> Consciousness loves itself outrageously and it is positively blissed
> out in the joy of its experiences. If it weren't so engrossed in the
> ecstasy of it all, it would, I'm sure, be awed, but awe can only be
> the emotional state of a passive on-looker and *passive* is not a
> word we can apply to consciousness. The closer we, as humans,

come to this emotional state, the nearer we come to living as life is truly intended to be lived.[4]

Now, you could say to yourself, "Well, why not keep *looking* but create patterns in The Field for a limited $10 million or $1 billion in my imaginary account? That would be fine with me." You could certainly create that if you wanted to, after crossing the Busting Loose Point, but why would you want to if you had full confidence in your Cosmic Overdraft Protection? Let me share an example to illustrate the importance of what I just said.

Suppose, to do *absolutely everything* you wanted to do in a given year, you'd need to express appreciation of $250,000 in the form of money—if you were to track the flow and count it all up. If your Cosmic Overdraft Protection would *cover* every check you wrote along the road to the $250,000, why would you need any more *income* that year? In Phase 1, you might answer by saying you'd use the additional *income* to do even more things, *pay* for *unexpected expenses* or unplanned *purchases*, sock it away for retirement, *save* it to do things in the future, and so on. But if you had *unexpected expenses* or wanted to do other things—in that year or in the future—your Cosmic Overdraft Protection would click in and *cover* those checks too. When you reached retirement age, your Cosmic Overdraft Protection would *cover* all those checks, too.

So, if you had Cosmic Overdraft Protection, why would you need any more money sitting in an account somewhere or appearing to flow in as income—now or in the future? You wouldn't. You also wouldn't have any need for a *net worth* of any size or significance. Why would it matter how much money you had piled up if all your checks for doing absolutely everything you wanted or needed to do would be *covered*?

Do you see how deep the rules and regulations of The Money Game run? The need to *earn* as much as possible, sock money away, build up as large a *net worth* as possible, and so on is all based on the illusion of scarcity in the available supply of money. Once you take the scarcity away by opening to your Infinite Abundance, the need for piling up money completely disappears.

| KEY POINT | **Limited is limited (no matter how big the numbers appear to get), infinite is infinite, who you really are is infinite and infinite is where you want to be after crossing the Busting Loose Point.** |

So here's the question I have for you. I asked it once before from a different perspective but I'm asking again now, since your X-ray vision has been turned on for a while. If you could only choose one or the other, what would you choose:

- An unstable and artificial state of limitation—no matter how big the numbers appear to get—and the need to manage, track, count, and measure the flow of money
- Your natural state of Infinite Abundance, Cosmic Overdraft Protection, and a truly unlimited supply of money with no need to manage, track, count, or measure anything

I chose option number two. Assuming you choose option number two as well, your life then becomes about asking and answering this question on an ongoing basis: What do I want to play with now, just for the sheer fun of playing? That's why I call playing The Human Game in Phase 2 being in creative ecstasy, and, as I explained, as you continue expanding and changing, you'll answer that question in different ways.

Let me give you a few specific examples of how this *can* look. A year ago, I woke up one morning and felt inspired to offer a brand-new live event called Busting Loose from The Money Game. I thought it would be fun to do. I created the illusion of the actual title and subtitle of the event (which I repeated in this book) coming to me fully formed in a meditation. So I scheduled the event. There was no analysis or thought about it. I just felt the urge to do

it so I did it. I didn't do it to make money. I didn't do it to help people (there's no one out there to help). I did it simply because I
wanted to do it and I thought where it goes, it goes. I scheduled
four days for the event without even knowing exactly what I'd say
or do during the four days. I also felt motivated to request $2,000
as an expression of appreciation from attendees.

You might ask, "If money doesn't matter, why request any appreciation at all?" If you had a thought like that, understand that it's
coming from an old Phase 1 *there's a limited supply of money available
and when I spend, I have less* mentality. Expressing appreciation is
one of the most natural and empowering forms of expression there
is, for reasons you now understand. It's a great gift to create an
opportunity to express—or receive—appreciation. Appreciation is
an acknowledgement of the value of a creation. Money is just the
symbol of that expression. This is a very subtle but important point
to really get.

At the time, I'd been getting very excited by the possibilities of
using multimedia tools (audio + video + text) on and off the Internet and had expressed appreciation for video production equipment and software to create incredibly cool productions. One day,
after scheduling the Busting Loose from The Money Game live
event, I thought, "Wouldn't it be fun to use my new equipment and
tools to create a multimedia invitation to the event instead of writing a sales letter like I used to do in Phase 1." So I did that. Acting
100 percent from what I felt motivated to say and show, I created a
multimedia invitation over a three-day period and had a blast
doing it. I had no concern about convincing anyone to come to the
event. Why? Because there's no one out there to convince in Phase
2, nor does anyone need any convincing. They're all just actors
helping me play my games. I created the illusion of inviting them
as I felt inspired to create it. It ended up being a 40-minute video
presentation. Interestingly enough, the presentation didn't clearly
explain what would happen at the event or what it was all about.
In fact, when the attendees actually arrived and I asked them to
raise their hands if they had no idea what the event would be about

but they just *felt* they needed to be there, virtually everyone raised their hands.

I then felt motivated to send out one e-mail to my mailing list about the event. Here's what it said:

> I'm writing today to invite you to join me at a brand new live event I'm producing in June. The event is called:
>
>> Busting Loose from The Money Game
>> Mind-Blowing Strategies for Changing the Rules
>> of a Game You Can't Win
>
> The title says it all so that's all I'm going to share with you at this time.
>
> If the event is right for you, I trust you'll feel drawn to click through and discover all the exciting details. Just click on the following link if you'd like to claim your multimedia invitation to this transformative new event.

In the past, while playing The Money Game in Phase 1, I would have written a long letter designed to compel or motivate or convince people to go to my web site and watch the video invitation. Not in Phase 2! I sent that specific e-mail out because I felt like sending it out. I didn't care if zero people came to the event, two people came, or 60 people came (which was the maximum the room I rented could hold). I didn't care if I made money on the event or not. Why? Because that's not what it was about or where my abundance comes from. Remember, I was "breathing" at that point.

I later felt motivated to send out a second e-mail to my list, but that's all I did to promote it. In Phase 2, there's no need for promoting anything although you can certainly create the illusion of promotion if it's fun for you. I knew everything surrounding the event would come from patterns in The Field, including how many people appeared to attend, who attended, and how they appeared to find out about it, so I felt no motivation to manipulate the hologram to create the illusion of a specific outcome. As it turned out, 28 people came from all over the world, and I had an absolute blast doing the event, as did they.

| KEY POINT | As you move more deeply into Phase 2, you continue taking life one moment at a time, living in reactive mode, following the lead of your Expanded Self, using the treasure hunting tools and following what brings you joyfulness.

At the time of this writing, I still enjoy teaching, writing, and using multimedia tools to create remote learning experiences and invitations into my orbit. Therefore, I've continued creating opportunities to do those things *in the manner I just described*. I may not always do that, but I'm doing it at the moment. I live the same way with everything I do—business and personal—including when I wake up and decide to hang out and watch movies all day or play with my kids or have special time with my wife or reach out to my friends. I'm absolutely thrilled to see where it goes as I continue applying the treasure hunting tools and moving more deeply into Phase 2.

For many years when I was in Phase 1, I said to people, "Had my life gone differently, I would have loved to be a movie director because I've always loved movies and the rich creative potential of the visual medium, especially now with what you can do with special effects." But I wrote it off and said "Not this lifetime. I chose a different path." Now that I've crossed the Busting Loose Point, however, I no longer write anything off. I know I can create anything from a pattern in The Field and pop it into my hologram to play with.

As I mentioned, as I was entering Phase 2, my fascination with video production opened up and grew. The fascinating thing is, never in my wildest imagination did I ever think my passion for the visual medium and my passions for Consciousness, teaching, and transformational work would ever merge. Yet, they appear to be merging at the time of this writing as I'm continuing to push the envelope on what's possible when using the visual medium to teach and play. Most importantly, it all happened without any conscious desire or intention on my part as the Persona. It just unfolded on its own. Who knows, I may still choose to create the illusion of directing a movie someday—a Hollywood film or some entirely new way of sharing transformational knowledge through visually communicated stories. Stay tuned!

Once you pass the Busting Loose Point, it'll look how it looks for you. As you open up more and more to who you really are, you'll experience whatever you experience. As I explained, there are no rules or formulas for how Phase 2 looks or unfolds. That's the really exciting part. I don't know what it's going to look like for you and it doesn't matter. As I explained, after you cross the Busting Loose Point, it's all about playing with what you want to play with, exactly how you want to play with it.

No matter what you may be thinking right now, imagine for a moment that everything I've shared in this chapter is true, real, and possible for you. Imagine you actually crossed the Busting Loose Point, opened into your Infinite Abundance, qualified for Cosmic Overdraft Protection, and were living in a state of creative ecstasy. If you were actually living in that space, would you still:

- Set goals?
- Care about the results you produce?
- *Worry* about your personal income or the profits in your business?
- *Worry* about where your next customer is going to come from or whether they can *afford to pay* for your product or your service if you're playing the business game?
- *Worry* about what to do in any situation?
- Care about *discounts* or buying *on sale*?
- Care about how much money you have piled up in your accounts?

ut your *income* or *net worth*?

ut the value of your *investments*?

- Care about the economy or stock market?

No, no, no, no, no, no, no, no, no, no!

Why? Because none of it would matter to you anymore. Why set goals when you can create anything you want for the sheer pleasure of playing with it? Results are irrelevant when you're playing the Phase 2 game after crossing the Busting Loose Point. There's no longer any scarcity of money or limitation of any kind. Once you've tapped into an unlimited supply of money through your Cosmic Overdraft Protection, what do any of the numbers matter? What does it matter what the economy or stock market appears to be doing? You're creating your own version of them in your hologram anyway.

Can you imagine how differently your life would flow and how differently you'd feel living this way? It boggles the mind, doesn't it? Yet, it's real and it's there for you if you do the Phase 2 work. Maybe it all still sounds like pie in the sky to you, but it isn't. If you think about it, based on everything I've shared with you in this book—the philosophy, the science, the Mechanics Of Manifestation, and all the stories I've shared—it's the logical extension of where you go when you cross the Busting Loose Point. Plus, as I've explained, there's no need to accept it on faith or take my word for it. You can and will prove it to yourself if you make the leap into Phase 2 and do the work with patience, commitment, discipline, and persistence.

Remember too that no matter how excited you may feel about what life can be like after crossing the Busting Loose Point, it pales in comparison to what the actual experience is like. I can't adequately express in words (though I did my best), the joyfulness, exhilaration, peace, relaxation, and freedom I experience as I breathe my abundance. As I explained in the Introduction, busting loose from The Money Game can't be described. It must be experienced.

Here's something else that's really cool about living in Phase 2 without limits or restrictions. *Other people* act as reflections of what you're thinking and feeling about yourself or beliefs you've energized, right? If you do the Phase 2 work, you expand, you open up, and your appreciation for yourself, your creations, and the magnificence of The Human Game skyrockets, what *must* happen? You must get tremendous appreciation reflected back to you from the *other people* in your hologram. It has to happen. It will happen in the form of money and also in the form of compliments, kindness, special favors, love, and gratitude.

Since I crossed the Busting Loose Point, the degree to which other people have increased their appreciation for me is staggering. It manifests itself in small ways, like differences in how waiters treat me in restaurants, how clerks treat me at retail stores, how flight attendants treat me on airplanes, and how front desk people treat me when I check into hotels. It also manifests in large ways like the way my wife and kids interact with me, the way Cecily's family and my family treat me, the way friends interact with me, and the way *other people* treat me when I create them to come play with me when I choose to speak, do live events, release remote learning tools, or write books like this one.

When I was playing the Phase 1 game, when I offered live events, home study courses, or books, for example, I always created a very polar response to myself and the material. There was always a group of people who would return products and ask for their money back, or ask for refunds from live events, saying they weren't satisfied. People would reject my ideas and say, "There's nothing new in that for me," or "That's just not my cup of tea," or "That violates my religious beliefs." In those days, my appreciation for myself was much lower than it is now. As a result, it had to reflect back to me in the way *others* treated me and responded to me.

That dynamic changed because of how much my appreciation for myself, my creations, the creative process, and The Human Game have risen. You'll see this too in your life, including in a business context if that's your passion right now. If you work within the illusion of a business environment and you use the treasure hunting tools consistently to reclaim power, re-affirm The Truth and dramatically increase your levels of appreciation, what *must happen* with bosses, associates, fellow employees, customers, and prospects? Their appreciation for you must rise! What could that increased appreciation look like? An unexpected financial bonus or promotion? Praise? Cool new opportunities? Awards? Does life become more joyous, fun, and fulfilling when the appreciation being expressed for you soars off the charts? You'd better believe it!

> **KEY POINT** **It's not possible for anyone to treat you badly, or reject you or anything you say or do in your hologram. All you can do is create the illusion of it and convince yourself it's real. Once those patterns collapse, nothing but the appreciation that's your natural state can be expressed by or to you.**

Do you see now why I had to give you all the puzzle pieces I did before we got to this chapter? If I didn't, you'd never have believed or understood the magic of the Busting Loose Point. Despite the foundation I laid for you in previous chapters, you may still have some doubts you'll need to reclaim power from. If you felt impatient with me at various points during earlier chapters and wished I'd hurry up and get to the point, perhaps you'll feel some appreciation now for why the book was created to unfold as it did.

You could probably put the book down now and feel like you *got your money's worth*, but there's still more. When you'd like to get some of your questions answered, questions I know you have and a few others you may not know you have yet, turn the page and continue on to Chapter 14.

The Dialogues

*Statistically, the probability of any one of us being here is
so small that you'd think the mere fact of existing would
keep us all in a contented dazzlement of surprise.*[1]

—Lewis Thomas, Physician and Essayist (1913–1993)

*The shoe that fits one person pinches another; there is no
recipe for living that suits all cases.*[2]

—Carl Jung, Psychologist

W hen I share the Busting Loose from The Money Game
material with live audiences, through Home Transformational Systems and Phase 2 coaching programs, participants have the opportunity to interact with me and ask questions as
they first discover the material and later as they apply the treasure
hunting tools in their daily lives.

Since that's not possible for you with this book, and since I want
to support you in receiving maximum benefit from the Busting
Loose Process and applying the treasure hunting tools, I compiled a

list of the most commonly asked questions and my answers for you in this chapter. Some questions and answers are short, others are long, and others reflect the back and forth of a conversation.

QUESTION: I'm still stumped about how I can take it one moment at a time and live in reactive mode when I have responsibilities like my job, spouse, children, friends, and family.

ANSWER: It's really quite simple and you're just making it seem complex as part of an old Phase 1 trick to keep you away from The Truth. When you have responsibilities, what does that really mean? It means you have decisions to make and actions to take every day. What did I say about Phase 2? You do what you feel motivated or inspired to do. That takes care of the action part. What did I say about decisions? You make the choice you feel motivated to make and trust it's perfect and you can't mess it up or make a mistake. In both cases, if you have discomfort, you apply The Process and continue applying it until there's no more discomfort around the decision or action. Then you do what you feel inspired or motivated to do. Its really simple, and you can do it no matter what your situation.

As to the being in reactive mode, your Expanded Self is going to pop plenty of opportunities into your hologram to support you in doing the Phase 2 work. You're going to be extremely busy responding to what gets popped in. You're certainly not going to be bored or have a shortage of things to do. And unlike a Persona in Phase 1 who might be careless, forgetful, or overwhelmed, your Expanded Self isn't going to take His or Her eye off the ball and starve or ignore your career or personal life. Everything will be just fine.

QUESTION: What about when people ask you to commit to something in the future or you feel like committing to something in the future? How do you live moment to moment then?

ANSWER: In Phase 2, you do what you feel motivated or inspired to do, before or after applying The Process to any discomfort you have about your decisions or possible actions. If an opportunity or request to do something in the future pops into your hologram, and you feel motivated to do it, you do it. I do it all the time. It seems like living this way is tough or impractical, but it's actually the opposite. It's much easier and more practical than typical Phase 1 living and decision-making strategies. However, you're still responding to opportunities that get popped into your hologram versus trying to *make something happen* in the future. Plus, I can't resist this opportunity to tweak with your head one more time. There is no future. Think about that for a minute. In Phase 1, there's the belief that the future is real, out there, tangible, solid, and it flows out of the present moment or is the logical extension of it. None of that is true. The Truth is: There's only a string of present moments that are created from very complex and interwoven patterns in The Field. If you look at the actual film a Hollywood movie is shown from, you see a series of single frames with one image on them. When a projector displays the film, those single frames get linked together and create the illusion of movement and continuity, but it's all just an illusion. It's the same thing with your hologram and as the patterns shift in The Field, so does your so-called future.

QUESTION: You said everyone else is our creation and we're giving them a script telling them what to say and do in our movies. So, if I don't like what they're saying or doing, if I don't like the script, what do I do? Do I argue with them? Ask them to do something else? What if I get mad at them?

ANSWER: The answer to this question has several layers. First, the natural inclination from Phase 1 beliefs is to argue with or get mad at people who aren't saying or doing what you want them to. From a Phase 2 perspective, you know you're giving yourself another opportunity. Imagine a movie is being filmed. Imagine the script for the movie calls for an actor named Joan to say, "I hate you!" to an actor named John, then slap him across the face and walk out of the room. Imagine the script just called for John to raise his palm to his cheek where he'd been slapped, say, "Ow!" and stare at Joan as she walked out of the room. Suppose, as the scene was being filmed, Joan told John she hated him, slapped him and walked out of the room. Would John then say to Joan "Why did you do that?" No, he knows why she did it. Would he say "Stop it, I don't like being slapped?" No. The script is the script and that's what the actors follow. If you don't like what someone else is saying or doing, you're uncomfortable, right? So you apply The Process. There's no *need* to express your discomfort to the other person. They're just following your script to give you a gift. Then after you apply The Process, either once or as many times as it takes, you then say or do what you feel inspired or motivated to say or do as it relates to the other person. If you do the Phase 2 work and reclaim power from the discomfort, you may very well find that person acting from a completely different script and therefore saying and doing completely different things.

There is a second layer to the answer. There are times, from my experience, when the script actually calls for you to argue with another actor in your movie because the arguing is supportive for you. For example, it may heighten the intensity of your discomfort and therefore the amount of power that's available to reclaim in that moment. So, despite what I just said, if you know you can apply The Process but you still feel motivated to argue with an actor in your hologram, do it and trust that the arguing is supporting you beautifully.

The third layer to the answer is that there are no rules or formulas for how to live in Phase 2, and you can't make a mistake or mess up if you trust what you feel genuinely motivated to say or do in the moment, all of which is being shaped by your Expanded Self from a pattern in The Field.

QUESTION: Where you are now on the Phase 2 journey, do *you* argue with the actors much?

ANSWER: More often than not, I choose to apply The Process to the discomfort and don't argue with actors when they support me in getting uncomfortable. I rarely see the need or benefit from it anymore. I find that once someone has said or done something, it stirs me up, and I apply The Process to it (once or many times), their behavior and actions change and there's no need to discuss it. They did what they did to set something into motion for me, and once it was set into motion and I did the Phase 2 work, there was no need for them to continue what they were saying or doing. And if they did, then I'd go back and apply The Process again, but still not engage with them about it. However, don't take that as a rule or formula. I don't. It's just where I am and what I do. I always trust and follow what I feel motivated to say and do.

QUESTION: Obviously, most of the people out there don't know about Phase 1, Phase 2, the treasure hunting tools, reclaiming power, or any of this. How do I deal with that huge gap in perception with friends, family, kids, spouse, fellow workers, and others?

ANSWER: I'll give you a general answer then get more specific. First, it's not necessary to discuss Phase 2 work or concepts with other people. You can do it if you choose, but understand it is not necessary. In Phase 2, other people are just actors who are saying and doing what you ask them to say and do to support you in using the treasure hunting tools. They can easily play their roles without conscious knowledge of Phase 2. If they need to know about Phase 2 and have a dialogue with you about it, the script will make the need and opportunity for that clear, then you can trust and flow with it. As I mentioned, when I first entered Phase 2, I didn't discuss it with my wife for six months. There were two reasons for that. First, as you can see from the unfolding of this book, it's not something you can do in a few minutes. There's a lot to share. Second, I didn't feel motivated to do it. As I moved more deeply into Phase 2, she asked me what I was doing because I seemed so different. Her question opened a doorway to start discussing it so I started discussing it at that point. She later came to a Busting Loose from The Money Game live event where she was exposed to the whole system. If I'd had this book at that time, I would have given her a copy. I have coaching clients who are couples where both are consciously aware of and playing the Phase 2 game with each other. I have other clients who are creating the illusion of doing it by themselves. I have clients who, like me, traveled the path alone for a while, then created others to join them. The most supportive choice for you will be made obvious by what pops into your hologram on a daily basis. If you feel motivated to share this with someone else, simply give them a copy of this book or, suggest they get one of my Home Transformational Systems, or, if I'm still doing them, suggest they attend one of my live events.

QUESTION: What if I talk about Phase 2 with someone and they tell me they think I'm crazy or have gone off the deep end?

ANSWER: No one else has any power or independent decision-making authority in *your hologram*. If you created a conversation like that, it would be coming from a script you handed the other actor and they would either be reflecting back a fear *you have* that this is all crazy (which is quite likely to surface in the beginning of your Phase 2 experience), or they'd be saying it to set something into motion to support you on your journey. In either case, just apply the appropriate treasure hunting tool and respond. It will take care of itself.

QUESTION: What if something bothers or scares you and you don't know why? Do you have to be able to label the belief or cause of the discomfort to apply The Process?

ANSWER: You don't need to label or have intellectual understanding of discomfort to apply The Process to it. Discomfort is discomfort. Just apply The Process to it.

QUESTION: Have you and your wife Cecily ever reclaimed power together on something?
ANSWER: No.

QUESTIONER: Is that something you'd consider at all?
ANSWER: There's no need for someone else to reclaim power from something in your hologram. They have no power in your hologram. Only you do. If I reclaim power from an egg, my hologram will shift and Cecily will shift along with it. If Cecily appears to be reclaiming power from something in my hologram, nothing is really happening in my hologram, although I could create the illusion of something happening if I choose.

In Phase 1 there's a belief that if multiple people get together and meditate or focus on something together, the group dynamic adds power to the equation and increases the likelihood of achieving the goal. For example, in a recent movie called *What the Bleep Do We Know*, one of the scientists described an experiment done in Washington, DC, relating to the high crime rate there. He explained how a large group of skilled meditators meditated on a particular day about peace in Washington, DC. He then described how the crime rate dropped significantly on that day, so much so that the police couldn't believe it.

That was a completely manufactured holographic scene. From a Phase 2 perspective, it's simply not true that the meditators decreased the crime rate. It's an illusion. Remember, there's no True cause and effect *in the hologram*. As part of playing The Human Game, people can certainly pop the illusion of a group dynamic appearing to add power to something, appearing to create a result in their holograms, and convincing themselves it's real. But it isn't real. Having said that, if it would be fun for you to create the illusion of reclaiming power from something with your spouse or someone else, you can certainly do it. You can't hurt anything by doing it. Just keep in mind what's real and True as you do it.

QUESTION: You said you'll know when you've crossed the Busting Loose Point. How do you know and what does it feel like?

ANSWER: You just know from deep inside yourself. It's like being smacked over the head with a two-by-four it's so obvious. Not painful like that would be, but as obvious as that would be. You'll see your thoughts, feelings, and behavior changing. You'll just notice yourself naturally ceasing to count and measure the flow of money in your life. You'll just notice yourself naturally expressing appreciation for your creations and letting the rest take care of itself. You'll feel no discomfort or limitation about money where you used to feel so much—no matter what you're looking at in your hologram. Believe me, it will be obvious, but it will look how it looks and feel how it feels for you as a unique Infinite Being. Remember, once you make that shift, you can't fall back again. When you make the shift, you make the shift.

QUESTION: You said that my Expanded Self takes great care of me, supports me perfectly as I play The Human Game in Phase 1 and 2. However, based on the painful experiences you described as being part of your Phase 2 journey and the stories you shared about the painful experiences of others, it looks like many of the things that may happen to me aren't what would be called favorable. Is that right?

ANSWER: *Not favorable* is a made-up Phase 1 concept and judgment. Everything that gets popped into your hologram is *favorable*, no matter how you choose to judge it, or it wouldn't be there. There aren't any accidents. Nothing is random. If it's happening, there's a pattern in The Field that your Expanded Self put there for a reason, with intelligence, and then popped it into your hologram. We all make up stories about what it means and whether it's *good* or *bad*. You remember the structure of eggs? Judgment is a big part of the eggs. We judge everything, sometimes *negative* and sometimes *positive*. In Phase 1, its slightly different, but in Phase 2, everything you call unfavorable is the exact opposite because it gives you the opportunity to reclaim huge amounts of power that translates into huge amounts of freedom and joy!

QUESTIONER: So when you described some of your Phase 2 experiences as excruciating, was that your judgment of it?

ANSWER: It was a description of how intense the pain appeared to be in the illusion at the time. I didn't say it was bad, but yes, it was excruciating in terms of how painful it appeared at the time. I was aware enough, at that point, to know there was great value in it. Part of me still hated it at the time, which was my judgment of it. Part of me still wanted it to go away, which was my judgment of it. But I was always simultaneously aware that it was a Phase 2 creation to support me in doing the Phase 2 work, so I did the work—over and over and over, day after day after day as I described.

QUESTION: How do I deal with all the things in my life that are still obviously Phase 1 illusions—washing the car, walking the dog, brushing my teeth, eating, going to work, playing with my kids, and so on.

ANSWER: This answer has multiple layers to it. Here's the first one. Nothing in the hologram is real, yet it appears absolutely real. The illusion is totally convincing. So, looking at it from that perspective, anything you do—no matter how big or small it appears—is a miracle, and enormous appreciation can be expressed for it and for yourself as the Creator of it. For example, if you brush your teeth, there are no teeth, there is no toothbrush or toothpaste, there is no water, there is no sink. If you wash the car, there is no car, no water, no soap, no wax, no sponge or rag, or spray nozzle. If you walk the dog, there is no dog, no leash, no road, no grass, and no poop or plastic bag in which to put it. If you eat, there's no food, no mouth, teeth, or chewing. It's all made up. Yet, it appears to be real and when looked at for the miracle it truly is from that perspective, every-thing is a supremely joyful experience. There's nothing to *deal with* (to use your wording) if you really look at it. You just do what you feel motivated to do.

As for going to work and playing with your kids, beyond what I just said, you just *deal with* experiences like that as you *deal with* all other Phase 2 experiences, taking it one moment at a time, being in reactive mode, and applying the treasure hunt-ing tools as appropriate. It's all just raw material that gets shaped to support you in doing the Phase 2 work.

Here's the second layer. There's no need to reclaim power from everything in your hologram, nor could you. Why would you want to reclaim power from a sunset, a beautiful ocean scene, or a forest, for example? They are illusions, yes, but illu-sions that provide joy and inspiration for you. You want to reclaim power from the creations that limit you, not all cre-ations. And you only want to reclaim power from the eggs your Expanded Self leads you to. For example, at this moment in time, I still brush and floss my teeth. I know my teeth aren't real and tooth decay isn't real, but my Expanded Self hasn't led me to reclaim power from my teeth at this time, so I continue brushing and flossing and going to the dentist. That may change one day. It may not. And remember, you're creating all of it.

At the time of this writing, I wear reading glasses. I know my eyes aren't real and my reading glasses aren't real, but my Expanded Self hasn't led me to reclaiming power from them yet, so I continue using the glasses which is beautiful support for that creation in its own way.

My Expanded Self did lead me to reclaiming huge amounts of power from The Money Game, The Emotions Game, and The Relationships Game and to apply the four treasure hunting tools and I've followed His lead. As time passes and I move more deeply into Phase 2, who knows what I'll be led to apply the treasure hunting tools to and where all of this may go. I don't know and I don't care. It's all magnificent.

QUESTION: Sometimes I have thoughts like this: "I don't know if this stuff really works. I don't know if this Phase 1/Phase 2/ Reclaiming power stuff is real or I've just been conned or am suckering myself with a sexy sounding philosophy. I don't know if this is working for me." How do I respond?

ANSWER: There are two parts to your question: doubts and wondering it if *works*. Let's look at both separately. First, what are thoughts like that really? Discomfort, right? So what do you do? Apply The Process to those feelings. Next, remember, in Phase 1, the goal was to keep yourself away from your power at all costs. What better way to keep yourself away than looking right at The Truth and convincing yourself it's false, it doesn't work, you're just conning yourself? It's a brilliant strategy and it works extremely well in Phase 1. When you have feelings like that, you're showing yourself how you fooled yourself in Phase 1 and also giving yourself the great gift of being able to reclaim lots of power from those illusions.

Finally, in Phase 1 there's the illusion of a direct cause-and-effect relationship between effort and results from that effort. That's what we mean when we say something *works* in Phase 1. In Phase 2, there's no such relationship. In Phase 2, as you know, you apply the treasure hunting tools to apply the treasure hunting tools and where it goes it goes. You have no agenda, no investment in outcomes, no desire to change, fix, or improve the hologram.

Let go of whether it appears to be *working* or not. As long as you judge, you continue feeding power to the illusion and you can't reclaim your power. As long as you look for proof, you're saying "I don't believe it's true," and if you say that, The Truth can't act like The Truth because there's still power in the limitation eggs. This is tricky but so important. I realize this is easier said than done, but it gets easier and easier and then very easy over time as you continue applying the tools and expanding.

Your hologram *will* change. It must change as you reclaim power and collapse patterns. But it changes as a natural outgrowth of doing the Phase 2 work. It doesn't change and cannot change simply because you want it to change or because you don't like something or you'd prefer something else for the reasons you now understand.

QUESTION: Sometimes, I have a hard time and it's confusing trying to figure out if a message or guidance or what I feel motivated to do is coming from my Expanded Self or from my Persona or the voice of a parent or mentor inside me. How can I get clarity on this?

ANSWER: How would you describe the feeling of not knowing where the guidance is coming from? Is there discomfort?

QUESTIONER: It's uncomfortable for me because I'm afraid of listening to the wrong guidance or message and making a mistake.

ANSWER: If it feels uncomfortable, you apply The Process to it. Period. No exceptions. It doesn't matter what the discomfort is or where it appears to be coming from.

QUESTION: You said to apply The Process as discomfort comes up. Is it ever advisable to write down all of the things I don't like, all the things I don't want, then apply The Process to them one by one, not with the agenda of getting rid of them, but just because I know they're points of discomfort I can reclaim power from?

ANSWER: You let your Expanded Self lead you to the eggs. You don't need to go looking for them. It's an old Phase 1 trick that you've got to make lists and systematically take action on it to make things happen. What pops up, you deal with. Why? Because your Expanded Self wants to show you where to place the strategic dynamite charges to collapse the building of your Phase 1 illusion. My experience in my own life and with people I've coached is your Expanded Self will keep you plenty busy once you commit to Phase 2, and you won't feel the need to go looking for opportunities to reclaim power. You may create a different scenario for yourself and that's fine. Phase 2 is about responding to what pops into your hologram and doing what you feel motivated or inspired to do—not because it makes sense logically, or it seems like the right or smart thing to do, or you feel obligated to do it. So in this example, if you truly felt a strong sense of motivation or inspiration to make a list like that (not because its an old Phase 1 creation and habit), follow the motivation, trust it, and do it.

QUESTION: I have a lot of voices in my head, self-judgment, self-criticism, and self-doubts. Will they go away once I reclaim enough power from the patterns creating them?

ANSWER: They will not go away if you try to make them go away for the reasons we discussed. You can't judge something and reclaim power from it as those are mutually exclusive activities. However, if you do the Phase 2 work day in, day out, without attachment or agenda, yes, they will drop out of your hologram as a natural byproduct of your expansion. You are a magnificent Infinite Being. It's not possible for you to judge, criticize, or doubt yourself. All you can do is create the illusion of those things and convince yourself they're real. When you drain the power from those creations and illusions, just like if you drain the power from any limited creation, the patterns collapse and the creation disappears from your hologram. It's an inevitable shift that takes place.

QUESTION: What about integrity, ethics, and morals?

ANSWER: You may not like or agree with my answer at first, but I'm here to tell you The Truth. From a Phase 2 perspective, integrity, ethics, and morals are Phase 1 creations. They're all made up. They're all illusions made to appear real, like everything else in your hologram. The same thing holds true if you look at it honestly and objectively from a Phase 1 perspective. Throughout history, people have tried to come up with a single moral code of conduct that could be applied through the centuries and across cultures. You know what? It's not possible. What we call integrity, ethics, and morals varies from person to person, time period to time period, culture to culture, and situation to situation.

QUESTION: You talk about Cosmic Overdraft Protection. You talk about just expressing appreciation for the creations you want to experience with total trust the money will take care of itself. Does that really mean if there's something you (the Persona) wants or needs you'd just buy it right away without checking the balance in your account at all? Or would you wait until you have in fact manifested the amount needed?

ANSWER: You're asking this question because you still have so much power invested in The Money Game—as you should at this point. However, once you cross the Busting Loose Point, you'd never ask that question. Once you cross the Busting Loose Point, you have absolute and total trust in who you really are, how much power you have, and that your Infinite Abundance is real and available to you. When you have that certainty, then yes, you'd just express appreciation for what you want and the money would be there for you, without checking balances.

It takes time to reach the Busting Loose Point and cross it. And once you cross it, if you're like me (and you may create something different), you'll continue reclaiming power and expanding what's possible for you. When I first crossed the Busting Loose Point, I was able to express appreciation for many creations in this manner, up to a point. However, because of the way I built my eggs in Phase 1, I noticed that if I considered expressing appreciation that way with *numbers* that got past a certain size, limiting beliefs would click in again and I'd get uncomfortable. So, I applied The Process to all such discomforts and continued expanding what was possible for me in this regard. As a result, what's now possible for me now has soared off the charts.

QUESTION: What about the subconscious mind everyone talks about and gives so much power to?

ANSWER: There is no subconscious mind. It's all a Phase 1 creation designed to support the illusion being real. Remember I said that all Truth must somehow be distorted or skewed in order for The Human Game to work in Phase 1? What people call the subconscious mind is like that. It's a distortion of The Truth of The Field, the Expanded Self, and Consciousness.

QUESTION: You say that you live in reactive mode in Phase 2, that you follow the lead of your Expanded Self to apply the treasure hunting tools without agenda, wants, goals, or outcomes. What about wants and desires? What about proactively creating things in Phase 2? Do we ever get to the point where we do that?

ANSWER: Your question is coming from Phase 1 beliefs about needing to be proactive, manifesting, and creating your own reality. There are no rules or formulas in Phase 2. You create whatever you want to create to play The Human Game the way you want to play it. As I said, my journey is far from over. I don't know where Phase 2 will ultimately lead for me, much less for anyone else. I have a theory on this I'll share with you. Speculation doesn't have much value in Phase 2 (it's a Phase 1 trick), but I'll share it with you anyway because you might find it valuable. At the start, Phase 2 is all about applying the treasure hunting tools. There's so much power to reclaim, so many patterns to collapse, so much expansion and appreciation to experience and enjoy, that proactively creating things isn't on the menu. It's like going to medical school in Phase 1. You're so busy learning about the body at the start you don't even think about performing surgery or treating a patient.

However, my theory is that as you move more deeply into Phase 2, proactive creation becomes possible. My theory is when that point is reached, different people will make different choices. Some will decide to proactively create illusions to play with, and others will continue to allow themselves to be surprised.

For example, returning to a story I shared in Chapter 12, I might wake up one morning and *decide*, I really want to have the experience of directing a movie. Then my Expanded Self might create that experience, allowing it to unfold over time to allow me to play with the creation in pure joyfulness. As the Persona, I wouldn't consciously be aware of every detail in advance because if I did, what fun would there be? My Expanded Self would still create the patterns, energize them, and pop them into my hologram for me to play with.

The other possibility, using the example I just gave, is I wouldn't decide I want to direct a movie, but by simply waking up every day and seeing what gets popped into my hologram, it would simply happen and be a surprise for me. That sort of surprise mode is where I'm living at the time of this writing, and I find the element of surprise to be quite delightful. I may continue living like that or I may unfold into something else as I continue expanding. In reality, if you look closely at the two examples I just gave you, there's isn't any significant difference between "deciding" to create something and being surprised by how it unfolds, and being completely surprised by all of it.

QUESTION: I'm still not getting why I should focus on or appreciate something that's not real. There's something missing from my mind-set here.
ANSWER: What isn't clear when you look at that?

QUESTIONER: The fact that it's not real. I don't see why I should put my attention or energy into appreciating it.
ANSWER: Do you like movies?

QUESTIONER: Yes.
ANSWER: Is a movie real, what you're seeing up on the screen?

QUESTIONER: On a certain level, it is.
ANSWER: Is it really? If someone's getting stabbed up on a screen, are they really getting stabbed?

QUESTIONER: No.

ANSWER: Okay. Can you appreciate how much effort went into it from the producer, director, actors, crew, animators, special effects people and all the other people, time, energy, and effort that went into creating it?

QUESTIONER: Certainly.

ANSWER: Just overlay that same idea onto your life. You're the director, producer, animator, special effects wizard, and star of the movie. You create the actors and actresses, the crew, the set, special effects, everything. You're making the whole production up in Consciousness and immersing yourself within it instead of sitting in a theater watching it. You're convincing yourself its real when it's all just smoke and mirrors. That's the space to get into. If you can appreciate what goes on behind the scenes to make a movie possible, you can easily appreciate what's going on behind the scenes to make your hologram appear real which is an infinitely more difficult task.

QUESTION: Have you taken moments from your past and applied The Process to them? Can you use it to deal with something from childhood?

ANSWER: Yes, but perhaps not in the way you mean. Again, there's no need to go looking for eggs to reclaim power from. You don't need to go back over your past, isolate events that appeared to cause you pain, and apply The Process to them. You apply The Process when discomfort naturally comes up, which means when your Expanded Self leads you to eggs and opens them up for you. As you do that, of course, you'll dive into discomfort that relates to your past. All your eggs were created and energized through the process of growing up.

I can tell you, however, that *from my experience*, when I apply The Process, I rarely have conscious awareness of an event or experience in my past that may be linked to it. I'm just immersing myself in the discomfort energy without thinking about what it is, where it came from, and so on. Analyzing things in that way, going back over the past, finding core caus-es of *pain*, and working with them consciously is a Phase 1 cre-ation and trick. There's no need to have conscious awareness of the cause of an egg unless knowing it supports you in playing The Human Game the way you want to play it. Then you may give yourself an insight, awareness, or a-ha. Your experience may be different from mine.

QUESTION: This is called Busting Loose From *The Money Game*, but this isn't really about money at all, is it? It's really about your entire life, isn't it?
ANSWER: Exactly! Yet a tremendous opening and expansion does come with money for the reasons you now understand. Howev-er, as you so wisely suggest, it goes way beyond money. Money is just the entry point to a form of expansion that expands out into your entire life.

Well my friend, our journey, for now, is almost at its end. You've received nearly all the pieces of the puzzle, the big picture has popped out into full view for you, and you can see it clearly. Now there's a decision to be made. When you're ready to consider what I call The Invitations, turn the page and continue on to Chapter 15.

The Invitations

Truth exists; only falsehood has to be invented.[1]

Georges Braque, Painter (1882–1963)

I think of life itself, now, as a wonderful play that I've written for myself. . . . And so my purpose is to have the most fun playing my part.[2]

—Shirley MacLaine

When I go to an amusement park and ride the roller coaster, it always starts out slowly. I slide into the seat, buckle my seatbelt, and wait for the ride to begin. Then the car starts moving, slowly at first, then faster, faster, and faster as it goes this way and that, uphill, downhill, around, and about. Then it slows down again and comes to a stop as it ends. As I unbuckle my seatbelt and rise to exit the ride, I feel exhilarated but also a bit disoriented from the wild ride I just took.

Does that describe the wild ride you just took? You started out with Jack Canfield's Foreword and my Introduction as you slid into your seat and buckled your seatbelt. Then you started moving slowly as you discovered the rules of the game. Then you started moving faster and faster, this way and that, uphill, downhill, around, and about as you discovered the philosophy, the science, Phase 1, Phase 2, the treasure hunting tools, and the Busting Loose Point. With the end of the last chapter, you slowed down again and you're about to come to a stop and exit the ride, perhaps feeling both exhilarated and a bit disoriented yourself.

So, as you prepare to return to your life, the obvious question is: What now?

First, the wild ride you took isn't for everyone. You wouldn't have created this book and popped it into your hologram unless one of the following is true for you:

- You're ready to enter Phase 2—now—and the book is acting as the *Launch Point.*
- You plan to enter Phase 2 soon and wanted to get your feet wet before reaching the Launch Point and leaping off it.
- You want to play the Phase 1 game a while longer but with enhanced awareness of The Truth about what's *really* going on.

If I was still playing in Phase 1 of The Human Game, I would be acting as if you, the Persona, had power in your hologram and I'd be saying its now time for *you* to decide what you want to do. But I'm playing the Phase 2 game, and I know the decision has already been made by your Expanded Self.

So what's the decision and how will you know? Time will tell. If this was your Launch Point into Phase 2, you'll know. You'll get what I call a "knock me over the head so I can't miss it" sign. You'll actually feel as if someone flipped a switch in your life and everything changed in that instant. You'll start seeing the weird things I discussed actually showing up in your hologram. You'll start experiencing unusual and intense discomfort and you'll feel a natural motivation to apply the treasure hunting tools in response.

If you're getting ready to make the leap into Phase 2 and wanted to get your feet wet first by exposing yourself to this book, things will appear to move the way they always did before you created this book, but you'll feel a subtle shift, a heightened level of anticipation and awareness of what's going on around you as you wait to arrive at the Launch Point—like an astronaut waiting to enter the rocket ship and take off on a journey into space.

If you want to continue playing the Phase 1 game a while longer but with enhanced awareness of The Truth about what's really going on, things will appear to stay pretty much the same for you, but you'll notice yourself seeing into the Phase 1 game with the X-ray vision I helped you turn on in Chapter 7. You can't take the wild ride you did and not leave it profoundly changed. It's just not possible.

KEY POINT **Whether you launch yourself immediately into Phase 2, you launch yourself soon, or you remain in Phase 1 a while longer, the answer to the question "Now what?" is the same. You do what you *feel* motivated or inspired to do, before or after applying The Process to any discomfort you feel.**

If you continue playing the Phase 1 game a while longer, I still invite you to apply The Process when you feel uncomfortable, either exactly as I explained it, or in slightly modified form with fewer steps and different language. As I discuss in my *Busting Loose from The Emotions Game* live events and Home Transformational System, emotions aren't something that happen to you, emotions are something you do. You choose how you feel at any given moment by how you choose to interpret and respond to the events you experience in your daily life.

In Phase 1, we create the illusion of being in the passenger seat with our emotions, with no control, just along for the ride, instead of being in the driver's seat, with full control and maneuverability. If you apply The Process to the discomfort you feel going forward, even if you continue playing the Phase 1 game, you can start moving into the driver's seat on the emotions that color your world. In short, you can start creating the illusion of feeling better as you continue playing the Phase 1 game.

If you accept my invitation to apply The Process while remaining in Phase 1, you don't need to accept or believe everything I shared in this book. You can simply dive into the middle of any discomfort you feel, as you would if applying The Process in Phase 2, feel it as fully as you can, acknowledge you created the discomfort by your own choice in response to the event that appeared to trigger it, and you can reclaim the power from it by simply affirming you're doing so. You can do that without acknowledging that you're an Infinite Being; that there's a Phase 1 and Phase 2 of The Human Game; that there's a hologram, power, The Field, patterns, or eggs. If you do this, you'll find the emotional landscape you experience in Phase 1 will change dramatically, and you'll also be well prepared if and when you do choose to enter Phase 2.

If you reach the Launch Point immediately or soon, you have your tool belt. You'll know when and how to use the treasure hunting tools that are on it and I have a different invitation for you that has five parts:

1. Patience
2. Remembering
3. Trust
4. Appreciation
5. Expansion

As I discuss each part of the invitation separately, bear in mind I'll be repeating several key points I've already made.

Patience

For purposes of discussion, the Phase 2 journey is divided into two parts. They actually occur simultaneously, but it's convenient to split them in half to discuss them. The first part is applying the treasure hunting tools to:

- Remember who you really are.
- Reclaim power.
- Reaffirm The Truth.
- Dramatically increase your appreciation for yourself as the Creator of everything you experience, your creations, and the magnificence of The Human Game.
- Give yourself a guided tour of how you fooled yourself so brilliantly in Phase 1.

As I explained, applying the treasure hunting tools to start playing The Human Game without limits or restrictions was *not* designed to be accomplished overnight. The tools were designed to be applied over time, taking as long as is needed to perfectly support yourself in playing The Human Game exactly the way you want to play it—and savoring each step in your expansion as you'd savor a fine wine, fine meal, novel, or play.

Consider this quote from Machelle Small Wright as you consider what I just shared:

> You are experiencing being on the threshold of change. It is quite difficult to relax during these times because "the threshold of change" means that one is still living out the old patterns but has vision into and is moving toward the new patterns. This makes him anxious to leave the old in order to fulfill his vision of the new. The resulting anxiety takes him out of step with the present and lessens the quality of the immediate steps one needs to move through in order to enter the vision of the new. Again, relax.[3]

Your experience may be entirely different, but if you're like me, despite your new knowledge and awareness, there may still be times when you get impatient, you want to make something you judge as "bad" go away or lessen in intensity, or you desperately want to get off the ride because it seems to get too wild for you. If that happens, and again—it may *not* for you—be gentle with yourself. Give yourself a break. Realize that judgments and feelings like that are perfectly understandable in the light of the transition that's taking place from Phase 1 to Phase 2. Simply apply The Process to your feelings of discomfort and allow it to take you where it takes you.

Remember

At all times, especially when the going appears to get tough, always remember three things:

1. *What's really going on:* You're reclaiming power, expanding, and changing in *huge* ways, even if it doesn't always look or feel like it.

2. *The Truth about the hologram in Phase 2:* Once you enter Phase 2, nothing in your hologram will have any significance, meaning, importance, stability, or solidity except to the degree to which it supports you in doing the Phase 2 work.

3. *Your ultimate destination:* Playing The Human Game without limits or restrictions is a treasure that's more valuable than any treasure you've ever heard about, read about, seen in the movies, or could possibly imagine from your current perspective. The little I sketched for you about what it's like pales in comparison to what's really possible for you in Phase 2.

If you're like me, and again, you may create something different for yourself, remembering those three key points will help you persist and continue doing the Phase 2 work even if part of you feels like throwing in the towel.

You'll also want to remember that you cannot judge a creation, hate it, dislike it, want to change it, fix it, improve it, or make it go away—*and*—reclaim power from it simultaneously. Those are mutually exclusive events. At the start of your Phase 2 journey, it's likely you'll still have many judgments as you're led to eggs to reclaim power from them. However, as you do the Phase 2 work, you'll see judgment naturally fall away as you continue to expand.

Remember that Phase 2 is not about logic, intellect, thinking, or trying to figure things out. It's about *feelings* and *direct experiences*.

You'll also want to remember that as you move more deeply into Phase 2, everything I've shared with you in this book, even the things you're certain you fully understand and "get," will become more and more real to you and your understanding and "getting" of it will deepen in ways you can't imagine right now. Look forward to these aha moments of expansion and remember to savor each one fully.

Trust

As quickly as you're able to do it, and you *will* be able to do it as you apply the treasure hunting tools and expand through the process, let go of the illusion of wanting to control or manipulate the hologram. Let go of the Phase 1 trick of needing to be proactive and taking massive action to make things happen or get things done. Let go of goals, agendas, investments in results, and outcomes. Trust your Expanded Self and simply follow its lead. Surrender into the Phase 2 game and allow your Expanded Self to lead you to the Treasure.

Appreciate

As Phase 2 unfolds for you, you're led to eggs in The Field, you reclaim your power from them, patterns collapse, and your hologram transforms—appreciate the magnificence of it all—you as the Creator of everything you experience, your creations, the entire Human Game, and the beauty and majesty of the Phase 2 expansion.

As your wisdom, power, and abundance expand, appreciate each moment of the opening and expansion. As more and more becomes possible for you in the hologram, appreciate those ever expanding possibilities.

As you experience discomfort, appreciate the gift it brings and the beautiful opportunity it gives you to reclaim your power. If the going appears to get tough and you feel fried, burned out, or overwhelmed, appreciate what a magnificent job you did of fooling yourself since it's not possible for you to feel that way—only to create the illusion of feeling that way and convince yourself the illusion is real.

As you see more and more of your magnificence unfold, appreciate yourself as the Persona and your Expanded Self (the Real You) for how well you supported yourself in playing The Human Game through Phase 1 and Phase 2.

As you shift into living in reactive mode, taking life one moment at a time, doing what you feel motivated or inspired to do—before or after applying The Process to reclaim power from discomfort—appreciate the simplicity of the Phase 2 game and how much more joyous and relaxing your experience ultimately becomes.

As you cross the Busting Loose Point, open to the Infinite Abundance that's your natural state and ultimately begin playing The Human Game without limits or restrictions, appreciate the magnificence of that achievement, and revel in the joyfulness and creative ecstasy you open into.

As you experience all of this and much more beyond what I've sketched out for you, if you feel like thanking me or appreciating me for writing this book and supporting you in making the leap into Phase 2, please redirect that appreciation and thanks back to yourself. You created the illusion of me and this book in your hologram to remind you of The Truth you always knew. This journey and the wild ride we took isn't about me. It's about *you*. I didn't "do" anything for you. You did it for yourself.

Expansion

As you've no doubt realized, this book isn't just about money. If you accept my invitation, leap into Phase 2, and use the treasure hunting tools as I've explained, you'll absolutely bust loose from The Money Game and begin "breathing" your Infinite Abundance.

However, the transformations in your Human Game experience won't stop there, as cool as that will be on its own. Expansion in Phase 2 isn't limited to money and abundance. It extends into every nook and cranny in your hologram. As I've suggested, by doing the Phase 2 work, you'll also see expansion and the potential for creating amazing and beautiful experiences in all areas of your life. You'll also give yourself opportunities to apply the treasure hunting tools to eggs that have nothing to do with money.

KEY POINT

Expansion in all aspects of your hologram is the name of the game in Phase 2.

You're now poised to begin the ultimate adventure available to anyone playing The Human Game. You're about to go on a hunt for a treasure more valuable than gold, more valuable than jewels, more valuable than all the oil buried deep in the ground, more valuable than the trillions of dollars on deposit in the banks of your hologram. You're on the brink of opening to power beyond anything you can imagine, joy beyond anything you can imagine, peace beyond anything you can imagine, fulfillment beyond anything you can imagine, abundance beyond anything you can imagine, and creative ecstasy beyond anything you can imagine.

No matter what your hologram looks like and no matter what level of discomfort you experience along the way, The Truth is, from the perspective of the Real You, you're having a blast. You're having the time of your life. You're in total bliss as you play The

Human Game exactly the way you want to in a universe entirely of *your* creation.

To hammer this point home, consider Hollywood movie makers again. If you're sitting in a movie theater watching a so-called horror movie, tragedy, or intense drama, where *bad* things appear to be happening to the characters, you may judge those experiences and think to yourself, "Oh, that's terrible!" But what was the experience of the movie makers as they made the movie and when they watched the final cut? Joy, appreciation, and satisfaction, right? They had the time of their lives making the film!

For example, when you see a character being stabbed and bleeding on the screen and think "Oh, that's awful," the Hollywood special effects wizard who created the illusion is thinking "Yes! Look how real the injury and blood look. I really nailed that one!" When you see a character who appears to be suffering, the actor playing the role is thinking, "What a great performance! So convincing. Way to go!" The same thing is true for you and your total immersion movie experience. No matter what you see or experience in your hologram, the Real You is having a blast and is saying, "Wow! I really pulled that illusion off. So cool. What fun!" As you use the treasure hunting tools and continue to expand in Phase 2, you'll feel more and more like that yourself.

My wife has a passion for doing and teaching yoga. When she teaches, she always ends her classes by holding her hands together in prayer position and saying one word: Namaste'.

She then continues by defining the word like this:

> I salute the Divine in you, that is the Divine in me, that is the Divine that is present in all beings, and it is in this way that we are all one.

That seems like a wonderful note on which to end this part of our journey together. Why do I say this *part* of our journey together? Because if you leap into Phase 2, immediately, soon or at a later date, I'm sure our paths will cross again.

See you at the movies. . .

Adding Fuel to the Fire

When you have a fire burning and you add fuel to it, the flames grow larger and stronger. When I share the Busting Loose from The Money Game material with live audiences and through my Home Transformational Systems, I either suggest or provide specific resources to support participants on their Phase 2 journeys beyond that first touch point with the work. I'd like to share those resources with you here as fuel you can add to the fire that's now burning within you, or soon will be. I have divided the resources into seven groups:

1. Key Points
2. Movies and Television Shows
3. Books
4. Live Events
5. Home Transformational Systems
6. Coaching
7. Mailing List

Key Points

Throughout the book, I highlighted what I called *Key Points*. As a unit, they represent the core foundation the Busting Loose Process rests on. If you'd like to have a list of all the Key Points so you can refer to them as a group, print them out and create wallet-sized reminder cards, post them in your environment to remind yourself of The Truth, or whatever use might support you on your journey, just visit my web site here:

http://www.bustingloose.com/keypoints.html

Movies and Television Shows

I find it helpful when integrating new ideas to have visual examples of what the new way of thinking and living can look like. That's why I recommend the following movies and television shows. You should be able to find them anywhere, but to make it easy to have them shipped to you, I've included links on amazon.com for you. Sometimes web links stop working over time so if any of the links below stop, just go to amazon.com and search for the titles that interest you.

The Truman Show

Throughout this book, I compared The Human Game to a movie. One of the best visual examples of how accurate that metaphor is and how deep it can go is this movie. If you've already seen it—recently or a long time ago—try watching it again from the perspective of what you now know. There's the main character, Truman, played by Jim Carrey, numerous actors and actresses, the director, and the crew of a television show. The relationship between Truman, the director, and the crew isn't a perfect fit for the relationship between you and your Expanded Self because manipulation, ego, and control issues are clearly being displayed. Let those inaccuracies go, edit them out of your awareness, and enjoy the rest of the movie.

So many things in the movie perfectly illustrate the concept of Phase 1, Phase 2 (the ending), not knowing you're in a movie, how your Expanded Self sets up and unfolds "scenes" in your hologram to support you on your journey, how everyone you see is an actor playing a role and merely saying and doing what they're asked to say and do, and so on.

Web site: http://www.bustingloose.com/truman

Field of Dreams

This movie starring Kevin Costner magnificently illustrates many of the concepts I discussed in the book including:

- The importance of following your inner guidance, no matter how illogical or crazy it may seem and no matter how much resistance you appear to see or get in the hologram.
- Trusting yourself and your awesome power.
- Tapping into your Infinite Abundance when you do the two previous steps.
- Being open to abundance coming from anywhere and at any time, even if it doesn't make logical sense.

Web site: http://www.bustingloose.com/dreams

National Treasure

As I explained, the process of reclaiming power and busting loose from The Money Game is the Treasure Hunt of the Century. Your Expanded Self will be giving you clues and helping you follow them to ultimately find "the treasure." As the hunt continues, sometimes you'll be confused, angry, dejected, or feel like giving up. You will find your treasure, but you'll need to be committed, persistent, and relentless, just as the Nicholas Cage character was in this movie as he pursued his own clues in search of his own treasure. This movie illustrates all of this, step by step, and it's *very* powerful if looked at from that perspective.

Web site: http://www.bustingloose.com/treasure

The Game

To "shock" your system into letting go of old beliefs and opening up to The Truth about who you are, how things really work, and how powerful you really are, your Expanded Self must support you by creating extremely intense experiences. To make those experiences effective, actors must play roles and you must be convinced that they, and the experiences they help shape, are "real." This movie, starring Michael Douglas, illustrates these concepts. I must warn you that the movie is very intense and somewhat dark in places, but watching what happens and sensing the energy moving through it will be very supportive for you on your Phase 2 journey.

Web site: http://www.bustingloose.com/thegame

The Matrix

You'll have to edit out certain Phase 1 aspects of this movie, too, but it's very supportive to watch it, or review it if you've seen it before—especially the early dialogue between the Morpheus and Neo characters—to reinforce how everything is an illusion. You can also compare Neo's journey from discovering The Truth, awakening to being "The One," and opening into enhanced awareness and power to your own journey and expansion in Phase 2.

Web site: http://www.bustingloose.com/matrix

The Thirteenth Floor

You'll have to edit out certain Phase 1 aspects of this movie to get to the gems, but it's very supportive to watch this movie to reinforce how real holograms can become and the "Wow Factor" that results from experiencing how real they can be.

Web site: http://www.bustingloose.com/floor

What the Bleep Do We Know?

You'll have to edit out many Phase 1 aspects of this movie, too, but it's very supportive to watch this movie or review it if you've already seen it, especially the interviews with the scientists, to reinforce how everything we experience is an illusion created by Consciousness.

Web site: http://www.bustingloose.com/bleep

Chihuly: The DVD Set

If you've never heard of Dale Chihuly, he's one of the pioneers and most successful artists using glass as a creative medium. On these DVDs, you'll see example after example of what it looks like to live with money being irrelevant to your daily life, and to live in a "creative ecstasy"—immersing yourself within and following what brings you the most joyfulness. This set is very powerful when viewed from that perspective. You'll also see how the twists and turns of his life were magnificently scripted to support him, every second, in reaching this amazing state and living full out within it—no matter what happens.

Web site: http://www.bustingloose.com/chihuly

Star Trek: The Next Generation

This television series, which ran over seven years, is rich with illustrations of Phase 2 concepts in action, fully or partially with some

Phase 1 distortion. If you like science fiction, you'd find it valuable to purchase the entire set and go through it over time. At a minimum, go to the following web page, note the episodes that have "the holodeck" in them and watch as many as possible to see what's possible with a hologram.

Web site: http://www.bustingloose.com/holodeck or visit www.startrek.com and search for the keyword "holodeck"

The series also has a character in it named "Q" who is a member of an advanced race called "The Continuum" that's composed of omnipotent beings. You might also want to visit the following web page to see all the episodes with Q in them and watch as many as possible to see an illustration of what it's like to play in The Human Game amusement park without limits or restrictions. The Q character is extremely mischievous and not a great example of what Phase 2 living is like, but watching his infinite power at work can be quite supportive.

Web site: http://www.bustingloose.com/q or visit www.startrek.com and search for the keyword "Q"

Books

The Field, *by Lynne McTaggart*

This book summarizes the latest research into The Field: what it is, how it works, and related additional scientific research. It's a very technical book, a difficult read for some, but you'll find it to be an invaluable resource if you want to go beyond what I offered in this book as it relates to the science.

Web site: http://www.bustingloose.com/field

The Holographic Universe, *by Michael Talbot*

This book is a very easy and entertaining read that goes into much more detail on the hologram metaphor. One of the most valuable aspects of the book is all the stories and illustrations of the holographic and "unreal" aspects of what we call "reality." I strongly urge you to pick up a copy immediately and dive right in.

Web site: http://www.bustingloose.com/talbot

Q

In addition to the *Star Trek* television shows with the Q character, there's also a line of books available you might find supportive.

Web site: http://www.bustingloose.com/qb

Cradle to Cradle, by William McDonough

In Chapter 13 I talked about playing The Human Game without limits or restrictions, and making up games no one has ever even thought of before. Bill McDonough is an amazing man and a friend of mine. He's not consciously playing the Phase 2 game (at the moment) but he's a great example of making up games to play that no one has even thought of before. This book summarizes many of the projects he's involved with and will be quite supportive and inspiring to you. The early part of the book brilliantly illustrates the limitation of Phase 1 and the rest describes the new games Bill created to play. Even the paper the book is printed on represents playing a game that's never been thought of before!

Web site: http://www.bustingloose.com/cradle

Live Events

You may be interested in attending or referring someone to one or more of the following live events I conduct to support or supplement what you gained from this book:

- Busting Loose from The Money Game
- Busting Loose from The Emotions Game
- Busting Loose from The Relationships Game
- The Business School of Consciousness
- Busting Loose from The Body Game

To get details and schedules for these events and others that may be announced from time to time throughout the world.

Web site: http://www.bustingloose.com/schedule.html

Home Transformational Systems

You may be interested in ordering one or more of the following systems that were culled from my live events and enhanced for experiencing in the privacy of your own home. You may also want to refer someone you know or care about to one or more of them:

- Busting Loose from The Money Game
- Busting Loose from The Emotions Game

Other Home Transformational Systems may be released from time to time. To stay in the loop, visit the site.

Web site: http://www.bustingloose.com

Coaching

I offer a Coaching Program for people who want personalized support from me on their Phase 2 journey. There are group programs and one-on-one programs. From a Phase 2 perspective, when you join a Coaching Program like this, I become your creation and through me, you actually have a direct conversation with your Expanded Self and tell yourself what you really want to hear but prefer to hear from someone who appears outside of you. I had a Coach when I first entered Phase 2 and found it to be one of the most extraordinary experiences I've ever had. It was absolutely invaluable on my journey.

Web site: http://www.bustingloose.com/coaching.html

Mailing List

If you'd like to join my mailing list, stay in touch, and receive e-mail notification of opportunities within my sphere of influence, visit here and click on the little image that pops up when you get there.

Web site: http://www.bobscheinfeld.com

NOTES

Introduction

1. Roberto Cotroneo, "When a Child on a Summer Morning," in *Inkheart* (as cited by Cornelia Funke; Somerset, UK: Chicken House, 2003), p. 235.
2. Joseph Whitfield, *The Eternal Quest* (Roanoke, VA: Treasure Publications, 1983), p. 120.

Chapter 1: The Rules of the Game

1. Grady Claire Porter, *Conversations with J. C.* (New York: High View Publishing, 1985), p. 22.

Chapter 2: The Three Haunting Questions

1. *Bits & Pieces* (Chicago: Ragan Communications, 2005).
2. *Bits & Pieces* (Chicago: Ragan Communications, 2003).
3. Barbara Dewey, *The Creating Cosmos* (Inverness, CA: Bartholomew Books, 1985), p. 86.
4. See note 3, p. 92.
5. Sol Stein, *How to Grow a Novel* (New York: St. Martin's Press, 1999), p. 8.
6. See note 5, p. 10.

Chapter 3: Leaving Hollywood in the Dust

1. William Shakespeare, *As You Like It*, Act 2, Scene VII.

Chapter 4: The White Knight Comes Riding In

1. John A. Wheeler, April 16, 1990 speech at the Santa Fe Institute, as reported in Tor Norretranders *The User Illusion* (New York: Penguin Group, 1998), p. 10.
2. Michael Talbot, *The Holographic Universe* (New York: Harper-Collins, 1991), p. 1.
3. Barbara Dewey, *Consciousness and Quantum Behavior* (Inverness, CA: Bartholomew Books, 1993), p. 9.
4. Amit Goswami, PhD, Speaking in the movie *What the Bleep Do We Know?* (Twentieth Century Fox, 2005).
5. See note 3, p. 24.

Chapter 5: How Money *Really* Gets Created

1. Judy Garland, Speaking as Dorothy in the movie *The Wizard of Oz* (Warner Home Video, 1939).
2. Michael Talbot, *The Holographic Universe* (New York: Harper-Collins, 1991), p. 158.

Chapter 6: Mirror, Mirror on the Wall

1. Barbara Dewey, *As You Believe* (Inverness, CA: Bartholomew Books, 1990), p. 82.
2. Albert Einstein, quoted by Howard W. Eves, *Mathematical Circles Adieu* (Boston: Prindle, Weber, & Schmidt, 1977).
3. See note 1, p. 9.

Chapter 7: Turning on Your X-Ray Vision

1. *Bits & Pieces* (Chicago: Ragan Communications, December 2004).
2. *Bits & Pieces* (Chicago: Ragan Communications, February 2005).

Chapter 8: The Treasure Hunt of the Century

1. *Bits & Pieces* (Chicago: Ragan Communications, November 2004).

Chapter 9: Jumping into the Driver's Seat

1. *Bits & Pieces* (Chicago: Ragan Communications, November 2004).
2. *Bits & Pieces* (Chicago: Ragan Communications, July 2005).

Chapter 10: Putting Your Foot on the Gas

1. *Bits & Pieces* (Chicago: Ragan Communications, August 2005).
2. *Bits & Pieces* (Chicago: Ragan Communications, March 2005).

Chapter 11: Busting Loose

1. *Bits & Pieces* (Chicago: Ragan Communications, March 2005).

Chapter 12: Postcards from the Road

1. *Bits & Pieces* (Chicago: Ragan Communications, September 2004).
2. *Bits & Pieces* (Chicago: Ragan Communications, July 2004).
3. William Shakespeare, *Hamlet*, Act 1, Scene V.

Chapter 13: Playing without Limits or Restrictions

1. *Good Stuff* (Chicago: Ragan Communications, 2004).
2. *Bits & Pieces* (Chicago: Ragan Communications, January 2004).
3. *Bits & Pieces* (Chicago: Ragan Communications, January 2004).
4. Barbara Dewey, *Consciousness and Quantum Behavior* (Inverness, CA: Bartholomew Books, 1993), p. 27.

Chapter 14: The Dialogues

1. *Bits & Pieces* (Chicago: Ragan Communications, January 2006).
2. *Bits & Pieces* (Chicago: Ragan Communications, January 2006).

Chapter 15: The Invitations

1. *Bits & Pieces* (Chicago: Ragan Communications, May 2005).
2. *Bits & Pieces* (Chicago: Ragan Communications, October 2005).
3. Machelle Small Wright, *Dancing in the Shadows of the Moon* (Warrenton, VA: Perelandra, Ltd., 1995), p. 155.